D0596126

DRIVE LIKE HELL

DRIVE LIKE HELL

NASCAR'S BEST QUOTES AND QUIPS

Compiled by ERIC ZWEIG

FIREFLY BOOKS

A FIREFLY BOOK

Published by Firefly Books Ltd. 2007

First printing

PUBLISHER CATALOGING-IN-PUBLICATION DATA (U.S.)
Zweig, Eric, 1963-
Drive like hell : NASCAR's best quotes and quips / Eric Zweig.
[176] p. : col. photos. ;   cm.
Includes index.
Summary: An illustrated compilation of sarcastic,
wise, witty and humorous quotes about NASCAR racing.
ISBN-13: 978-1-55407-273-6 (pbk.)
ISBN-10: 1-55407-273-5 (pbk.)
1. Stock car racing – United States — Quotations, maxims, etc. 2. Stock car racing — United States – Humor. 3. NASCAR (Association). I. Title.
796.72/0973 dc22   GV1029.9.Z945 2007

Library and Archives Canada Cataloguing in Publication
Drive like hell : NASCAR's best quotes and quips / compiled by Eric Zweig.
Includes index.
ISBN-13: 978-1-55407-273-6
ISBN-10: 1-55407-273-5
1. NASCAR (Association)—Quotations, maxims, etc. 2. NASCAR
(Association)—Humor. I. Zweig, Eric, 1963-
GV1029.9.S74D75 2007   796.72   C2007-900273-0

Published in the United States by
Firefly Books (U.S.) Inc.
P.O. Box 1338, Ellicott Station
Buffalo, New York 14205

Published in Canada by
Firefly Books Ltd.
66 Leek Crescent
Richmond Hill, Ontario L4B 1H1

Cover and interior design by Sari Naworynski

Printed in Canada

The publisher gratefully acknowledges the financial support for our publishing program by the Government of Canada through the Book Publishing Industry Development Program.

For Jack, who loved cars, and for Stacey too.

CONTENTS

INTRODUCTION

"I feel like I got a pile of cattle chasing my ass, and I'm pedaling as hard as I can to stay in front of 'em. I'm looking behind me driving like hell."

Rusty Wallace

I like that quote. Sure, it's where the title of this book comes from, but it's more than that. In just two sentences, this quote encompasses the essence of NASCAR. It's the thrill of modern racing – with a hint of the stock car's "good ole boy" roots.

NASCAR (National Association for Stock Car Auto Racing) was formed in 1947. The "Strictly Stock" division (which has become the circuit we know today) started in 1949. But stock car racing is much older than that. Its roots date back to the Prohibition era of the 1920s and 1930s. (Even as late as 1941, stock car legend Lloyd Seay was killed in a dispute over illegal whiskey. Longtime NASCAR president Bill France Jr. has referred to him as "the Dale Earnhardt of 1941.") Obviously, running whiskey from hidden stills to hundreds of markets across the U.S. Southeast was a dangerous business. The drivers needed fast cars and a lot of guts.

Eventually, as the moonshine drivers got more and more competitive, they took to racing. And fans came out to watch them.

Today, of course, NASCAR has expanded well beyond its original Southern fan base. But then again, stock car racing has always had fans in far-flung places. Growing up in Toronto in the 1970s, we had racing at Pinecrest Speedway and, in the 1950s and 60s, there was stock car racing in the Stadium at the Canadian National Exhibition, where the CFL's Toronto Argonauts and later the Toronto Blue Jays played.

I got my earliest stock car experience attending Saturday night races at the Barrie Speedway in Ontario. It was lots of fun, and even on nights when we weren't at the races, you could hear the roar of the engines at our family cottage some three miles away. I still hear the roar on Saturday nights and it always makes me smile. The Barrie Speedway is the kind of place that current NASCAR driver Greg Biffle is referring to when he says, "running under the lights at the local short track, that feels like home."

I think what I liked about the stock car races even then, although I was years away from getting my license, was that these looked like cars anyone could drive. They weren't like Indy cars and Formula One racers. These were the cars you saw on out on the road – only with cooler paint jobs!

But of course, it's a lot tougher than it looks. As sportswriter Peter Golenbock says, "If baseball is chess with a bat, ball and glove, stock car racing is chess on wheels."

But you don't often get 100,000 fans screaming at a chess match. You didn't get 100,000 fans at the Barrie Speedway either. Still, I understand it when Kurt Busch says, "the coolest thing is when you come to a race ... when you see it live and you get the sound and you get the feel and then the smell."

Let's be honest. You won't get that here. But I had a good time putting this book together. I hope you'll enjoy it too!

"I want to be in this sport a long time, so I don't pay much attention to age. I just know it's gonna hurt someday when the young guys start passing me."

JEFF GORDON, AFTER BECOMING THE YOUNGEST WINNER OF THE DAYTONA 500 AT AGE 25 IN 1997

"Listen, it all comes down to the car and equipment you got. Here, if you ain't got it, you ain't going nowhere."

51-YEAR-OLD BILL ELLIOTT ON WHY AGE DOESN'T MATTER IN NASCAR

"I just can't see where [age] comes into play whatso-ever. Skillwise, it shouldn't make any difference at all. If you're 50 or 51 years old, you are as willing and ready to go to the front as the 21-year-olds are."

50-YEAR-OLD DALE JARRETT

"Racing in [NASCAR] has gotten a lot more physical the last 10 to 15 years, and you have to be in better shape. But I don't read what people write about me. I just go to the track every Sunday and try to be the best driver I can be."

51-YEAR-OLD BILL ELLIOTT ON CRITICS WHO WONDER WHEN HE'S GOING TO RETIRE

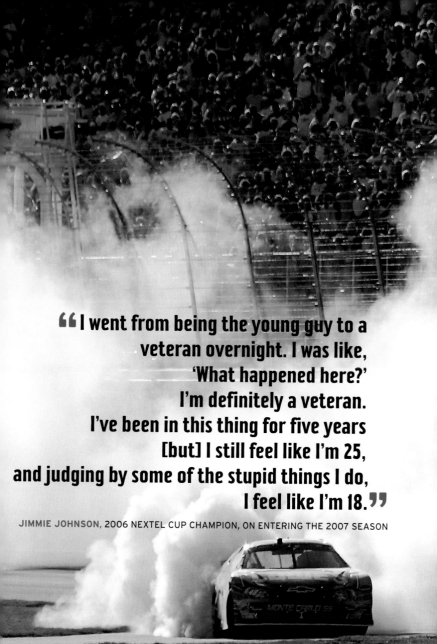

"I went from being the young guy to a veteran overnight. I was like, 'What happened here?' I'm definitely a veteran. I've been in this thing for five years [but] I still feel like I'm 25, and judging by some of the stupid things I do, I feel like I'm 18."

JIMMIE JOHNSON, 2006 NEXTEL CUP CHAMPION, ON ENTERING THE 2007 SEASON

"I'm winning races, I'm competitive. I'm seventh in points, and they talk about being over-the-hill. If I was 30th in points and not making races and not being competitive, I could understand them saying I'm over-the-hill or I'm ready to quit or whatever."

DALE EARNHARDT

"I'm not over-the-hill yet. I still love this. I still have nerve. Hopefully, I showed I have the skill left."

GEOFFREY BODINE, AFTER FINISHING SECOND IN THE DAYTONA 500 IN 2002. HE HAD WON THE DAYTONA 500 IN 1986, BUT HAD NOT COMPETED IN THE RACE SINCE 1999

"I knew there would be some seniors that would be interested, but I didn't know it would be as over-whelming as it has been. I signed more autographs than in my whole 20 years of racing."

JAMES HYLTON WHO, ALTHOUGH HE ENJOYED THE ATTEMPT, FAILED TO QUALIFY FOR THE 2007 DAYTONA 500 AT AGE 72

"People are going to get older and young guys are going to come in and race and get more competitive."

DALE EARNHARDT

"We were thinking of putting a younger driver in it, but I'm seasoned now. I might just drive it myself. Why should I let a young driver get in my brand-new car?"

JAMES HYLTON, WHO AT AGE 72 DIDN'T QUALIFY FOR THE 2007 DAYTONA 500, BUT WHO HOPED TO HAVE A CAR READY TO RUN AT BRISTOL

"Personally, I'd like to drive forever. Realistically, I know I'm not going to be able to."

KYLE PETTY ON HIS DECISION TO TAKE A FIVE-RACE MID-SEASON BREAK FROM DRIVING THE NO. 45 CAR TO WORK AS A NASCAR RACE ANALYST FOR TURNER NETWORK TELEVISION IN 2007

"The car doesn't know how old you are or how much you weigh."

51-YEAR-OLD KEN SCHRADER ON THE MANY YOUNG DRIVERS IN NASCAR

"Those were the old, fun days of racing. It's changed. There's more money in it and the cars are shinier. But overall, it's four tires and a brain. And young squirts blowing the old guys off the track."

FRED LORENZEN, WHO HAD 26 WINS IN 158 RACES BETWEEN 1956 AND 1972

"My dad's pretty special. I still remember the day
he told my mother I was gonna race at NASCAR's
fastest speedway. Daddy was spearing a piece of
meat at dinner. Looking away from her he said,
'Pass the potatoes, Eula Faye. Sterling's running
at Talladega this weekend.'"

STERLING MARLIN, ABOUT HIS FATHER COO COO MARLIN,
ONE OF THE MOST COLORFUL DRIVERS IN NASCAR HISTORY

"It's hard to say a lot about your brother, especially
in front of him. When the chips were down, Daddy
said we were going to work together, so that's the
way it was. I think if you look at the history of this
sport, you'd have to say Maurice was the best
engine builder there's ever been in NASCAR."

RICHARD PETTY, AT THE BANQUET FOR HIS BROTHER
MAURICE'S 2007 INDUCTION INTO THE NATIONAL
MOTORSPORTS PRESS ASSOCIATION'S HALL OF FAME

"We don't really spend much time together, but we do care for each other and we love each other to death. Yet, we want to beat each other into the ground at the racetrack, seeing who's going to come out on top."

KURT BUSCH ON HIS RELATIONSHIP WITH HIS
BROTHER KYLE

"The line in Vegas? 50 to 1, 10 to 1, I don't know. My mom always puts money on me. I tell her not to, but I'm glad she did today."

LAS VEGAS NATIVE KURT BUSCH AFTER COLLECTING HIS
FIRST NASCAR WINSTON CUP SERIES VICTORY AT THE 2002
FOOD CITY 500 AT BRISTOL

"In Friday's qualifying race, my daughter Bonnie said a prayer for me while I was leading. The next lap I wrecked, and that had been weighing on me the last couple of days. I'd hate for any child to think her prayers went unanswered, and that had bothered me the last couple of days."

BOBBY ALLISON AFTER WINNING THE 1978 DAYTONA 500

"It is pretty interesting that two brothers from the small town of South Boston, Virginia, both made it to the Winston Cup. It has brought us a lot closer together and gave us a better understanding of each other. I like racing with my brother every weekend, but I don't enjoy racing against him."

JEFF BURTON ON HIS BROTHER WARD

"We are very fortunate to both be able to race at this level, and we get to spend a lot more time together at the racetrack than we would if we had other professions. But, racing against your brother complicates things just a bit. You try extra hard not to have anything happen while you're racing each other. We wrecked each other a long time ago when we raced at the local track, and the wrath from our dad was enough to make sure it never happened again. There isn't extra pressure from him [Jeff], but I want to beat him just like I want to beat anybody else on the track."

WARD BURTON ON RACING AGAINST HIS BROTHER JEFF

"Lee Petty was the smartest driver I ever saw. When I raced Daddy, he beat me like a dang drum."

RICHARD PETTY ON HIS FATHER LEE, AN EARLY NASCAR STAR

"After Dad saw that I was serious about racing, he gave me his full support, as he would have done regardless of what I had chosen to do."

DALE JARRETT, A SCRATCH GOLFER WHO HAD CONSIDERED TRYING TO MAKE A CAREER ON THE PGA, ON HIS DECISION TO FOLLOW HIS FATHER NED INTO RACING

"The most intense, hard-driven man I have ever known."

NED JARRETT (FATHER OF DALE JARRETT) ON RALPH EARNHARDT (FATHER OF DALE EARNHARDT)

"I always wished I could race with my dad."

DALE EARNHARDT, WHO ONLY RACED AGAINST HIS FATHER RALPH ONCE, ADMITTING THAT ONE OF THE JOYS OF THE 2000 NASCAR SEASON WOULD BE THE CHANCE TO RACE EVERY WEEK WITH DALE JR.

"I don't plan on ever matching my father's accomplishments. I just came into the sport and race every lap. I enjoy racing. I have success. I feel like I'm one of the better drivers in the series at this point in my career. I feel like I'm a smart race-car driver. I really feel like I have achieved personally everything that I have wanted from the start. I've gotten everything that I've wanted. I wanted to come in here, be competitive, win races, make a living, and be able to go home and be satisfied with what I've done and that's where I'm at."

DALE EARNHARDT JR.

"Cotton Owens was leading and Daddy was second. They came up on me and I moved over to let them pass. Cotton went on, but Daddy bumped me in the rear and my car went right into the wall."

RICHARD PETTY

"I guess it will sink in once I see my daddy's eyes next week."

DALE EARNHARDT JR. ON CAPTURING THE 1998 BUSCH CHAMPIONSHIP

"Since I was a kid, I've dreamed about battling to the wire, finishing 1–2 with my dad. The only difference was, I wanted him to finish second."

DAVEY ALLISON, AFTER FINISHING SECOND BEHIND HIS FATHER BOBBY AT THE 1988 DAYTONA 500

"It don't mean s--- right now. Daddy's won here 10 times."

DALE EARNHARDT JR., WHEN ASKED HOW IT FELT TO CAPTURE HIS FIFTH CAREER TALLADEGA VICTORY IN 2004 (NASCAR FINED JUNIOR $10,000 AND DOCKED HIM 25 POINTS FOR SWEARING ON TELEVISION)

"My grandfather is the King, my dad is the Prince. I guess that makes me the butler."

ADAM PETTY, FOURTH GENERATION NASCAR DRIVER

"God created bumpers and ... bumpers were made for bumping!"

DALE EARNHARDT

"A lot of drivers get spooked by running wheel-to-wheel at 180 miles per hour and beating on each other. As far as hitting the other car, you can do it just as good at 180 as at 100 because there's only a mile or two per hour difference between the two cars. As long as you don't hit something that's standing still, you're all right."

RICHARD PETTY

"I hope he chokes on that 200 grand."

DARRELL WALTRIP, AFTER RUSTY WALLACE BLATANTLY SPUN HIM OUT WITH JUST TWO MILES REMAINING, WHICH COST HIM THE $200,000 PRIZE AT THE 1989 WINSTON AT THE CHARLOTTE MOTOR SPEEDWAY

"If a man thinks this is a leisurely Sunday afternoon ride, he ought not to be in the race."

RUSTY WALLACE, AFTER SPINNING DARRELL WALTRIP OUT OF FIRST PLACE AND GOING ON TO WIN THE 1989 WINSTON AT THE CHARLOTTE MOTOR SPEEDWAY

oil
OR OIL & LUBRICANTS

Holley
P CARBS

NASCAR
CUP S

BUD
POLE AWARD

MECHANIX WEAR

JESEL

McDonald's

Gillette MACH3 Turb

"The only way he was gonna beat us was if we wrecked —so he came up there and took us out himself."

MATT KENSETH AFTER A CRASH WITH DALE EARNHARDT, JR.

"I'd say he definitely had the better car and he was probably going to win the race. I killed his chances of doing that."

DALE EARNHARDT JR. REFERRING TO HIS WRECK WITH MATT KENSETH

"I'd be crazy to drive up on the rear of somebody and just spin them out in front of God and everybody."

> RUSTY WALLACE, DENYING THAT HE INTENTIONALLY SPUN DARRELL WALTRIP OUT OF FIRST PLACE EN ROUTE TO WINNING THE 1989 WINSTON AT THE CHARLOTTE MOTOR SPEEDWAY

"Everyone thinks Michael is a good guy. He is not the good guy like he acts like he is. Caution was out, and he wrecked me."

> ROBBY GORDON, AFTER HURLING HIS HELMET AT MICHAEL WALTRIP'S DOOR AT NEW HAMPSHIRE, THE CHASE'S FIRST RACE IN 2005

"We had the best car on the long runs, but I hate to win a race that way."

> JEFF GORDON, WHO BUMPED MATT KENSETH LATE IN THE RACE TO CLAIM HIS 75TH CAREER VICTORY AT THE 2006 SHEETROCK 400 AT THE CHICAGOLAND SPEEDWAY

"I know it was intentional."

> MATT KENSETH'S REACTION AFTER THE RACE

"For such a good kid with a great future, he made an awful stupid move."

TODD BODINE, AFTER 22-YEAR-OLD JEFF GORDON BUMPED
HIM AND CAUSED A SEVEN-CAR CRASH AT THE 1994
DAYTONA 500

"I never forget. Only thing is, when I smash back, he won't finish."

JIMMY SPENCER, WHO FINISHED SECOND TO KURT BUSCH AT
THE 2002 FOOD CITY 500 AT BRISTOL, AFTER BUSCH BUMPED
HIM TO REGAIN THE LEAD WITH 55 LAPS REMAINING

"If he wants to race that way, we can race that way. He ain't gonna push me around."

JOHNNY SAUTER, ADMITTING THAT HE INTENTIONALLY
PUNTED MATT KENSETH OUT OF HIS WAY ON THE FINAL
LAP TO WIN THE 2003 FUNAI 250 AT RICHMOND

"If you mess with me, you get messed with. I want to race you clean, I want to race hard, but if you're going to mess with me, then we're going to play, that's the way I look at it."

DERRIKE COPE

"Don't hit him! I know you can hear me, and NASCAR said that they are watching you."

DALE EARNHARDT INC. VICE PRESIDENT **TY NORRIS**, ATTEMPTING TO TALK DALE EARNHARDT JR. OUT OF PAYING BACK KURT BUSCH FOR AN EARLIER WRECK

"You're breaking up, man. I still can't hear you."

JUNIOR'S REPLY

"I've hit guys before, guys I've lapped a bunch of times who didn't belong out there racing. You can bend fenders in stock car racing without killing one another."

RICHARD PETTY

"I'm not mad, but it was a foolish thing to do. I was minding my own business when he started bumping. I was running as fast as I wanted to go and if he wanted to pass, he could. I just locked up my brakes and busted his radiator. I guess all we proved is that the back end of a Pontiac is tougher than the front end of a Ford."

NASCAR LEGEND GLENN "FIREBALL" ROBERTS, AFTER
BUMPING WITH FRED LORENZEN THROUGHOUT THE 1962
OLD DOMINION 500 AT MARTINSVILLE

"In a 200-lap race, there's no need to stick your neck out and take a chance. A couple of cars were faster than us, but they ended up a bunch of sheet metal in the garage. I think they made a mistake."

DAVEY ALLISON, AFTER STERLING MARLIN, BILL ELLIOTT
AND ERNIE IRVAN COLLIDED TO SET OFF A 14-CAR
ACCIDENT THAT CLEARED THE WAY FOR ALLISON TO
WIN THE 1992 DAYTONA 500

"My go-kart experience over the winter paid off, because I didn't let off the floor and we just kept hitting things and the wall and bouncing off everything. But man, this is the Daytona 500. Can you believe it?'"

KEVIN HARVICK, AFTER WINNING A FRANTIC, WRECK-FILLED 2007 DAYTONA 500

"This Stewart guy, man, I'll tell ya I don't know what's going on there. He's coming down the back straightaway with his finger out the window and just giving me the bird all the way down the straightaway after he'd run me through the fence. I'd like to take that finger and jam it right up his rear end, I'll tell ya that ..."

RUSTY WALLACE, AFTER HE AND TONY STEWART HAD BUMPED EARLY IN THE 2004 AUTO CLUB 500 AT FONTANA IN CALIFORNIA

"I don't know why they settle this stuff on the racetrack. I guess they're too scared to settle it outside the racetrack."

JEREMY MAYFIELD, WHO WAS KNOCKED OUT OF THE FIRST RACE IN THE INAUGURAL CHASE FOR THE NEXTEL CUP IN 2004, AFTER ROBBY GORDON SPUN GREG BIFFLE IN RETALIATION FOR AN EARLIER INCIDENT

**"Kevin spun me out.
We're supposed to be teammates,
but it doesn't seem that way right now."**

JEFF GREEN, UPSET THAT RICHARD CHILDRESS RACING
(RCR) TEAMMATE KEVIN HARVICK HAD SPUN HIM OUT OF A
RACE AT RICHMOND IN MAY OF 2003. GREEN WAS FIRED BY
RCR TWO DAYS LATER

"Of all the people to take you out, your teammate.
That was just lowdown, nasty, dirty driving."

SCOTT PRUETT (WHO CAME BACK TO FINISH FIFTH) AFTER
JUAN PABLO MONTOYA BUMPED HIM OUT OF TOP SPOT EN
ROUTE TO HIS FIRST NASCAR VICTORY AT A 2007 BUSCH
SERIES RACE IN MEXICO CITY

"It is just incredible to think that we're the best race team for a year. It's almost hard to put into words what I feel for these guys, how much I love them, and what a job that they've done week in and week out."

DALE JARRETT AFTER WINNING THE 1999 WINSTON CUP

"A championship is a very big notch in a driver's belt when it comes time for the next endorsement deal and the next sponsorship deal and so forth. And a championship is also a great hedge against your inevitable decline in performance. You can extend your career longer with that kind of success because you can market yourself as a champion."

ROUSH RACING PRESIDENT GEOFF SMITH

"If I can win races and win championships, I feel like my future is going to be OK."

DALE EARNHARDT, WHOSE SEVEN WINSTON CUP CHAMPIONSHIPS TIE HIM WITH RICHARD PETTY FOR THE MOST NASCAR TITLES

"Great champions ... are the ones who have won more than one championship. That's something that is very, very hard to do. I'm very proud to be able to say that I've won one and it's quite an accomplishment, but to be able to say I've won more than one is something even greater."

JEFF GORDON WHO, AFTER WINNING THE WINSTON CUP IN 1995, WON THE TITLE AGAIN 1997, 1998 AND 2001

"Being a champion, it's the only thing I ever wanted to be."

JIMMIE JOHNSON AFTER WINNING THE 2006 NEXTEL CUP

"You can take all the victory trophies and stuff them into a corner. I want the trophy that comes with the championship."

CHAD KNAUS, CREW CHIEF FOR JIMMIE JOHNSON, WHOSE FOUR 2006 VICTORIES AT THE TIME INCLUDED THE DAYTONA 500 AND THE BRICKYARD 400

"I think you can go out there and you can have a good day. You can hit it right on one day ... But to win a championship, you've got to do it throughout the whole year. You can't just hit it every once in a while, you've got to have it all the time and have the consistency – you can't fall out of races."

JEFF GORDON AFTER WINNING HIS FIRST WINSTON CUP TITLE IN 1995

"You can't ever get to the point where you think that you're just always going to have success. The best way to handle success is to act as if you haven't done as much as you need to do and to understand that you haven't done as much as you need to do. There's always more to do and there's always a way to do it better. There is no pinnacle. There is no end. If you've won a championship, then damn, there are people who have won two. And if you've won two, there are people who have won three. There is no place where you can get and say I've done everything that I've ever wanted to do. There's always more to do and there's always more challenges and there's always a way to do it better. That's the best way to handle it."

JEFF BURTON ON HANDLING SUCCESS

"It's the same thing this week as it was at the Daytona 500. You don't wake up one morning and say to yourself, 'Hey, I've got to do good now.'"

MARK MARTIN, HANGING ON TO 10TH PLACE IN THE STANDINGS THROUGH 24 OF 26 RACES IN 2006, EN ROUTE TO THE 10-RACE CHASE FOR THE NEXTEL CUP

"Here's the moral of the story: the next 10 races is the same 10 races that we had last year. You go to the track, you race and you get points for it. When it's over with, they'll tell us exactly where we finished in the points standings."

TONY STEWART, AFTER QUALIFYING FOR THE INAUGURAL CHASE FOR THE NEXTEL CUP IN 2004

"We're excited about these last 10 races. It's that kind of effort that we had tonight that we're going to put out every weekend for the next 10 weeks. If that doesn't get it done, then the other guys can have it. But we're not going to give up this thing without a fight."

JEFF GORDON, AFTER QUALIFYING FOR THE INAUGURAL CHASE FOR THE NEXTEL CUP

"I guess what matters is that we made it. We won
the battle, but we haven't won the war. We'll get
our guns polished up for the last 10 races and do
what we have to do as a team to stay focused and
take the right race cars to the right racetracks and
make the right calls. The driver will try not to
make any mistakes and make sure we don't have
any DNFs, engines failures and mechanical problems and go from there."

RYAN NEWMAN ON BEING THE 10TH AND FINAL QUALIFIER
FOR THE INAUGURAL CHASE FOR THE NEXTEL CUP

"I think we've got a great chance. We've got a lot of
really good tracks coming up. With this new
format, Lady Luck has got to be on your side to do
it. One DNF, and you're out of luck."

JIMMIE JOHNSON, AFTER QUALIFYING FOR THE INAUGU-
RAL CHASE FOR THE NEXTEL CUP

"Obviously, we're not happy about being 10th, but
we've got 10 races to get into first."

RYAN NEWMAN ON BEING THE FINAL QUALIFIER FOR THE
CHASE IN 2004

"We're in the best position in some respects, because the worst we can be is 10th. It's just a situation where we'll go out and do the things we've always done – that's qualify well and race well. We'll see where the situation stands at Homestead."

RYAN NEWMAN ON BEING THE FINAL QUALIFIER FOR THE CHASE IN 2004

"If I'm one of the guys [not in the top 10], it boils down to how much of an a-hole or how much of a friend that guy is. If I want to do him a favor and give him a spot, and I like him, then I'm gonna do it. But if he's a jerk, I'm going to make him work for it."

DALE EARNHARDT JR., SPECULATING ABOUT THE DRIVERS WHO DID NOT QUALIFY FOR THE INAUGURAL CHASE FOR THE NEXTEL CUP IN 2004

"As long as it's the same for everybody, and as long as the guy with the most points wins, versus the guy with the least points, the theory is still the same."

TONY STEWART ON THE RULE CHANGES MADE TO THE CHASE FOR 2007 (12 DRIVERS, MORE POINTS FOR WINS)

"In the past, I feel, it's been a lot more about consistency, and this year it's going to be a little bit more about winning. But in order to win the championship, you're going to have to do both."

KASEY KAHNE ON THE CHANGES TO THE CHASE IN 2007

"You could have put 20 cars in there last year and Jimmie Johnson was still going to win the championship because he ran better than everybody else."

KEVIN HARVICK ON EXPANDING THE CHASE TO 12 CARS IN 2007

"If you don't cheat, you look like an idiot; if you cheat and don't get caught, you look like a hero; if you cheat and get caught, you look like a dope. Put me where I belong."

DARRELL WALTRIP

"They haven't caught me if I am."

JUNIOR JOHNSON, WHO'S CHEVY WON NINE POLES AND SEVEN RACES IN 1963 — INCLUDING THE DAYTONA 500 — WHEN FORD ACCUSED HIM OF CHEATING

"I loved the game. Maybe I'd have four or five new things on a car that might raise a question. But I'd always leave something that was outside of the regulations in a place where the inspectors could easily find it. They'd tell me it was illegal, I'd plead guilty, and they'd carry it away thinking they caught me. But they didn't check some other things that I thought were even more special."

JUNIOR JOHNSON

"Ninety percent of the so-called cheating that was innovated, it wasn't cheating. There was no rule on how big the gas line could be. Everyone else ran a 5/8-inch gas line. That was adequate to supply the race engine with gas, no question about it. I chose to run a two-inch gas line, which was obviously much too big, but it was 11 feet long and it held five gallons of gas. **Nobody ever specified size.** A week after the race, the gas line couldn't be over a half-inch in diameter. The day that I did it, it was not illegal.**"**

EARLY NASCAR OWNER AND LEGENDARY MECHANIC **SMOKEY YUNICK** DISCUSSING A CHEVROLET HE ENTERED AT THE DAYTONA 500 IN 1968

"They will find out there is no way to police creativity. No way in hell! There's always some guy who comes along like Ray Evernham that's smarter than the average cat, and he's going to figure out a way to get around it. The difference between Gary Nelson's ability to think and Ray Evernham's – well, probably there's not a lot of difference in their IQs, but Evernham concentrates on engines and certain areas with a lot of expensive, very educated help. For 60 hours a week, he's studying new stuff to beat the rules. Gary Nelson is spending 50 hours a week trying to enforce the rules that were made yesterday. They're not even in the same game."

EARLY NASCAR OWNER AND LEGENDARY MECHANIC SMOKEY YUNICK WHOSE OWN INNOVATIONS WERE OFTEN CONSIDERED CHEATING

"That's baloney, man. That's what's wrong with America now. Every time somebody screws up, we tell them it's all right. You don't pay your bills? You can file bankruptcy. You kill somebody? Spend 10 years in jail, and we'll let you out. That's what's wrong with society now, man. If you do the crime, do the time. If you had the guts to do it, have the guts to take your punishment."

CREW CHIEF MICHAEL MCSWAIN, TELLING THE RICHMOND TIMES-DISPATCH HE WAS TIRED OF HEARING COMPETITORS WHINING AFTER BEING CAUGHT CHEATING

"NASCAR had a meeting three weeks ago. They just told us right there in the meeting that they weren't tolerating people going over the line and that the fines were getting bigger, the suspensions getting bigger, so everybody knew what to expect when they got here."

> TONY EURY SR., CREW CHIEF FOR ROOKIE PAUL MENARD, ON THE CHEATING SCANDAL PRIOR TO THE 2007 DAYTONA 500

"To not have another stretch like this."

> NASCAR PRESIDENT MIKE HELTON, WHEN ASKED WHAT HE HOPED TO ACCOMPLISH WITH THE HARSH PENALTIES HANDED OUT DURING THE CHEATING SCANDAL PRIOR TO THE 2007 DAYTONA 500

"I've just been happy through qualifying that we haven't been a part of it. It just crushed me when I found out that we were going to be right in the middle of it all."

> JEFF GORDON, WHOSE FAILED INSPECTION WAS DEEMED TO BE INADVERTENT, BUT STILL SAW HIM BUMPED FROM 3RD TO 42ND IN THE STARTING GRID DURING THE SCANDAL-PLAGUED LEAD-IN TO THE 2007 DAYTONA 500

"You've got to conduct yourself properly if you're going to play on the big stage. We're competing now with the NFL, and, I think, ahead of most other sports – the NBA, Major League Baseball, NHL, we're the equivalent or better. So we've got to conduct ourselves with integrity. That's what they're doing."

TEXAS MOTOR SPEEDWAY PRESIDENT EDDIE GOSSAGE
ON NASCAR RESPONDING TO THE CHEATING SCANDAL
LEADING UP TO THE 2007 DAYTONA 500 WITH FINES,
SUSPENSIONS AND POINTS DEDUCTIONS

"Somebody will cheat again. And somebody will get busted again. That's just the nature of things. Just because the NFL calls a penalty for holding doesn't mean that nobody's going to hold ever again. It's just the nature of competition, sadly."

TEXAS MOTOR SPEEDWAY PRESIDENT EDDIE GOSSAGE

"If you ain't cheatin', you ain't tryin'."

OLD NASCAR EXPRESSION

"To tell you the truth, I think he got off easy.

think it gave the sport a black eye. We've got to recover from that. **"**

E **NEMECHEK** ON THE FINES ($100,000), SUSPENSIONS (INDEFINITE) AND NTS DEDUCTIONS (100) HANDED OUT TO MICHAEL WALTRIP'S TEAM IN E WAKE OF THE CHEATING SCANDAL PRIOR TO THE 2007 DAYTONA 500

"Racing cars is not the safest thing. Maybe at times it's not the sanest thing."

MICHAEL WALTRIP

"I closed my eyes and turned the wheel and don't know how I didn't hit anything."

KURT BUSCH, AFTER SPINNING ON LAP 152 OF THE 2004 BANQUET 400 AT THE KANSAS SPEEDWAY

"It's amazing what you can do with your eyes closed."

BUDDY BAKER, WHEN AN INTERVIEWER PRAISED HIS SKILLFUL DRIVING THROUGH A SMOKE SCREEN FULL OF WRECKED CARS

"There's no bigger surprise than to be tooling along at 200 miles per hour and suddenly getting hit from the rear."

DARRELL WALTRIP

"I love Darlington in the springtime, I love Darlington in the fall. I love Darlington in the winner's circle, but I hate Darlington in the wall."

DARRELL WALTRIP, SINGING TO THE TUNE OF "I LOVE PARIS" AFTER HE HIT THE WALL TWICE AT THE 1989 SOUTHERN 500 AT DARLINGTON AND LOST OUT ON A MILLION-DOLLAR PAYDAY

"It was like dropping a sheet over your sunglasses. I had a small peephole and at the speed I was going, it was exciting. It might not have seemed exciting to you guys, but it was to me."

A.J. FOYT, THREE-TIME INDY 500 CHAMP, WHOSE ONLY REAL CHALLENGE IN WINNING THE 1972 DAYTONA 500 WAS WHEN JIM HURTUBISE'S CAR BLEW ITS ENGINE ON THE FINAL LAP AND COVERED FOYT'S WINDSHIELD WITH OIL

"Dirt. Smoke. Dust. I don't know what happened."

STACY COMPTON, AFTER A 19-CAR PILEUP AT DAYTONA

"If racing were completely safe, everyone would do it, and it wouldn't be a sport."

TIM FLOCK

"Racing is supposed to be dangerous. It always has been dangerous and hopefully always will be dangerous. If it were not dangerous and did not require a certain level of skill, then everybody would do it and there would be nobody left to fill the grandstands."

NEIL BONNETT

"Driving a race car is like dancing with a chainsaw."

CALE YARBOROUGH

"If the lion didn't bite the tamer every once in a while, it wouldn't be exciting."

DARRELL WALTRIP ON THE DANGER IN RACING

"Auto racing, bull fighting and mountain climbing are the only real sports ... all others are games."

AUTHOR ERNEST HEMINGWAY

"Don't come here and grumble about going too fast. Get the hell out of the race car if you have feathers on your legs or butt."

DALE EARNHARDT

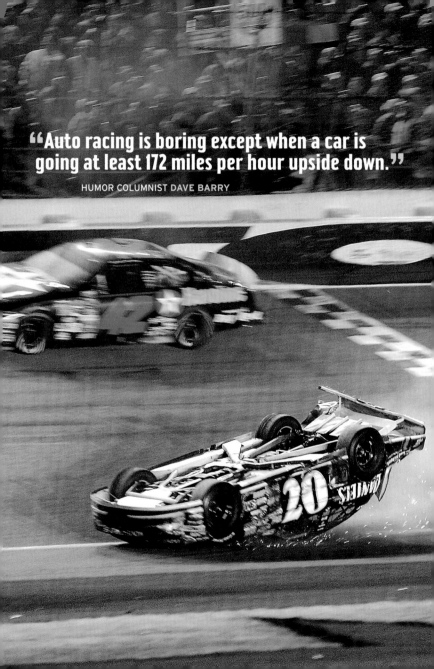

"Auto racing is boring except when a car is going at least 172 miles per hour upside down."

HUMOR COLUMNIST DAVE BARRY

"I'm a full-blooded racer. That's all I eat, sleep or drink. Whether it be in a Busch car or Winston Cup car, racing is what I want to do. I hope I can do it forever. For me to be able to live a dream tickles me pink. There's no room for error, and if you make a mistake, there's no telling what it'll cost you."

JOE NEMECHEK

"I was just born to be wild. I tried to be a nurse, a pilot and a beautician and couldn't make it in any of them. But from the moment I hit the racetrack, it was exactly what I wanted."

LOUISE SMITH, THE FIRST WOMAN IN NASCAR (IN THE 1940s AND 1950s)

"I don't even know that many movie stars. John Wayne's not here, so I don't know."

RICHARD PETTY, WHEN ASKED TO CHOOSE SOMEONE TO PLAY HIM IN A MOVIE

"So much of my life is spent just focused on driving race cars."

JEFF GORDON

"My job is to drive that black No. 3."

DALE EARNHARDT

"When you're a race-car driver, it's hard for me to go and watch. I love to go to the racetrack and be a part of it, but it is hard to go to the racetrack and not be involved in it."

FORMER DRIVER ERNIE IRVAN

"When I was 20 and ran my first race, I told myself I don't know how I'm going to do this for a living. I don't have the money to do it. But it is what I want to do."

DALE JARRETT, NASCAR VETERAN AND 1999 WINSTON CUP CHAMPION

"Do you think you'll be driving a race car for the rest of your life?"

BOB NODOLF, WHO WAS MATT KENSETH'S DRIVER-EDUCATION INSTRUCTOR IN HIGH SCHOOL, RELATING A STORY HOW KENSETH ONCE GOT SCOLDED BY HIS ENGLISH TEACHER FOR SKIPPING A CLASS

"Ya gotta wanna."

DICK TRICKLE

"I would have won a lot more if it hadn't taken me until 1960 to realize there was more to racing than horsepower. We usually had the fastest car, but in those early days, we were probably 10 years ahead of the tires, and I would wake up many a time after dreaming about the two booms – first the tire and then the car into the wall."

EARLY NASCAR OWNER AND LEGENDARY MECHANIC
SMOKEY YUNICK

"Today they race on highways. Back then, we had plowed fields."

TIM FLOCK

"When I began car racing back in 1946, it was just something to do. We did it because we loved to race. They called those little old cars we drove 'modifieds,' but we really didn't know a whole lot about modifying them."

COTTON OWENS

"I had done my homework on knowing how to drive a car when I ran hauling moonshine. I had to deal with revenue agents, the sheriff, the ABC [Alcohol Beverage Control] officers – all kinds. To be able to outrun them and keep from getting caught, I had to be very skillful, and that's what I did. When I showed up at the racetrack, that's just exactly what I'd been doing for several years. So I did have one up on the competitors."

JUNIOR JOHNSON ON HIS EARLY DAYS

"I had a steering wheel break on me at the Charlotte Fairgrounds once, and I drove with a pair of vice grips the rest of the race. Just clamped them down on the car and turned with the grips. It didn't go as fast as normal, but I finished the race."

EARLY NASCAR LEGEND BUCK BAKER

"It was the dustiest place I've ever seen. When the race started, it looked like someone had dropped a bomb."

TRACK OWNER CLAY EARLES ON THE FIRST STOCK CAR RACE AT THE MARTINSVILLE SPEEDWAY ON SEPTEMBER 7, 1947

"They told me if I saw a red flag to stop. They didn't say anything about the checkered flag. I wondered where all the cars were and then as I was all alone on the track, I noticed them all in the pits. They finally threw the red flag and I pulled in. I had finished third."

LOUISE SMITH, THE FIRST WOMAN DRIVER IN NASCAR
(IN THE 1940s AND 1950s)

"When we started, my pleasure was, the reason I did it, was I'd like to step out on the line Sunday morning and pull my pants up and say, 'Let's have a race.' If I won, I was happy. And if I didn't, I was already thinking about what I was going to change next week to beat their ass."

EARLY OWNER AND LEGENDARY MECHANIC SMOKEY YUNICK,
WHO BELIEVED THAT NASCAR HAD BECOME TOO MUCH
ABOUT ENTERTAINMENT AND NOT ABOUT RACING BY THE
END OF THE 1990s

"Years ago, you used to get out and fight and run around and chase each other with a jackhammer and stuff like that. Those were the good ol' days."

DALE EARNHARDT JR. JOKING ON THE DAILY SHOW WITH
JON STEWART

"We were having a ball. Nobody had ever run those cars before. It was real close, and you couldn't get away from anybody. **Guys didn't have safety belts.** One guy drove with a truck inner tube around him. **Another guy was tied in with a rope.** The cars were pretty much just like they came from the dealer. No roll bars. No nothing. No one had ever run brand-new cars, and people came out just to see what in the world was going to happen."

TIM FLOCK ON THE FIRST OFFICIAL NASCAR RACE, HELD AT THE CHARLOTTE SPEEDWAY ON JUNE 19, 1949

"Winning this award for the 11th time really says something about our fans. I have said it over and over, in this sport they stick with you no matter what."

BILL ELLIOTT, WHO HAS BEEN VOTED MOST POPULAR
DRIVER MORE TIMES THAN ANYONE IN NASCAR HISTORY

"Our fans would never waste good beer by pouring it on us."

JEFF GORDON COMPARING NASCAR FANS TO NBA FANS

"If it weren't for the fans, we wouldn't be out there in the first place, doing what we love to do. Every time I sign an autograph, it's like saying thank you to the fans for letting me do what I love to do, and make a living out of it."

RICHARD PETTY

"When we get to the track, we're basically turned loose to the masses. And you'd better be willing to deal with that politely, slightly, lightly, all nightly – whatever it takes."

DARRELL WALTRIP

"When it's time to go, I'll go. Until then, I have
  nothing to lose."

EARLY STOCK CAR LEGEND "RAPID" ROY HALL

"When you start thinking too much about wrecks and high speeds, it's time to quit."

GLEN WOOD

"You can't live your life in fear of what's gonna
  happen next."

BUDDY BAKER ON THE DANGERS OF RACING

"Racing is like life. If you get up one more time than you fall, you'll make it through."

ALAN KULWICKI, WHO WAS KILLED IN 1993 IN A
SMALL-PLANE CRASH EN ROUTE BACK TO BRISTOL

"The good Lord doesn't tell you what His plan is, so all you can do is get up in the morning and see what happens next."

RICHARD PETTY ON THE DANGERS OF RACING

"I look at it this way: When it's your time to go, you're going."

DAVID PEARSON

"We won it! We won it! We won it! The Daytona 500 is ours!"

DALE EARNHARDT AS HE CLIMBED FROM HIS CAR AFTER
WINNING THE 1998 DAYTONA 500, HIS FIRST WIN AT THE
BIG RACE, DESPITE HOLDING THE LEAD IN 17 OF THE
PREVIOUS 19 RACES

"I was just working the mirror. I was working to keep the race car in front until somebody turned us over or we crossed the line first ... Nobody turned us over."

DALE EARNHARDT, WHO LED FOR THE LAST 60 LAPS EN
ROUTE TO FINALLY WINNING THE DAYTONA 500 IN 1998

"I'll admit it. My eyes watered up in the race car coming to take the checkered. It's something I've always wondered what it might feel like."

DALE EARNHARDT AFTER FINALLY WINNING THE BIG ONE
IN 1998

"Even Dale, who hates cigars, took a few puffs. So I saw him do two things that day that I had not seen him do before."

OWNER RICHARD CHILDRESS ON THE CELEBRATIONS
AFTER DALE EARNHARDT FINALLY WON THE DAYTONA
500 IN 1998

"I've said before that those things didn't bother me. I lied. You don't come that close to winning the Daytona 500 and not feel it. It hurt."

DALE EARNHARDT AFTER FINALLY WINNING THE
BIG ONE IN 1998

"It's kinda neat.
As much as he's meant to the sport,
he deserves it."

RUSTY WALLACE, AFTER DALE EARNHARDT FINALLY
WON THE DAYTONA 500

"I'm excited for him. He got the lead when he needed to, and from then on, he controlled the race. As many times as he's been so close, he deserves it."

JEFF GORDON, AFTER DALE EARNHARDT FINALLY WON
THE DAYTONA 500

"I woke up this morning, and I still don't believe I won the Daytona 500."

DALE EARNHARDT

"From a NASCAR standpoint, when I came along it was sort of a good old boy, good old South sport, and I would have said you're crazy that we would be racing Toyotas one day."

RICKY RUDD, WHEN ASKED IF HE WOULD HAVE BELIEVED EARLIER IN HIS CAREER THAT ONE DAY THERE WOULD BE TOYOTAS RACING IN NASCAR

"It's the first entry of a non-Amercian manufacturer, so it's going to be a historical day. And it's one more thing to pay attention to. They are the new competition and everyone will want to see what they've got."

DODGE CAR OWNER RAY EVERNHAM ON TOYOTA'S NASCAR DEBUT IN 2007

"Toyota has a lot of money, but as long as NASCAR keeps the rules where they are, I think we'll be in good shape."

OWNER RICK HENDRICK

"I'm as American as the next person that's here and I pay my taxes just like everybody else and I love this country. Toyota is a big part of the United States economy. They're going to put a lot of dollars in the sport, in promoting our sport, and that's going to be good for our sport as a whole."

DALE JARRETT ON RACING WITH TOYOTA IN ITS DEBUT SEASON OF 2007

"Toyota will not find that the established teams and manufacturers will wither in their path as has been the case where they've decided to engage elsewhere [in racing]. We're gonna go to war with them, and they should give us their best shot because we'll be back and giving as good as we take."

OWNER JACK ROUSH

"NASCAR will be more popular because [Toyota]
is here. And NASCAR is going to be more popular
because Juan Pablo is here. But Jack Roush doesn't
have a problem with Juan Pablo coming. Why is
he so mad about Toyota showing up? You can't
handpick who comes in your door. This is a global
society. Toyota is certainly welcomed here. I haven't
talked to one driver who thinks it won't be good
for the sport."

MICHAEL WALTRIP ON THE ADDITIONS OF JUAN PABLO
MONTOYA AND TOYOTA TO NASCAR IN 2007

"I wish we were at a place in our society where we
didn't have to talk about Juan Montoya because
he's not from here. It's sad that we're not there.
It's not a NASCAR issue; it's a society issue. At
some point, we've got to get past that. And I'll be
damn glad when we do."

JEFF BURTON ON JUAN PABLO MONTOYA

"It's hard to get sponsors for Mexican drivers. NASCAR is a very competitive series. To get in is not easy."

FORMER MEXICAN INDY CAR STAR ADRIAN FERNANDEZ, WHO HAS TRIED TO MAKE THE JUMP INTO NASCAR

"This is a learning process for me, and there's no rush for me to be perfect. But I am also not here for fun. This is serious business, and I plan on winning races."

JUAN PABLO MONTOYA ON HIS MOVE FROM FORMULA ONE TO NASCAR

"It's huge for the Latin community and for everybody who supported me. Every time I'm out there I want to shine."

COLOMBIA'S JUAN PABLO MONTOYA AFTER GAINING HIS FIRST NASCAR VICTORY AT A 2007 BUSCH SERIES RACE IN MEXICO CITY

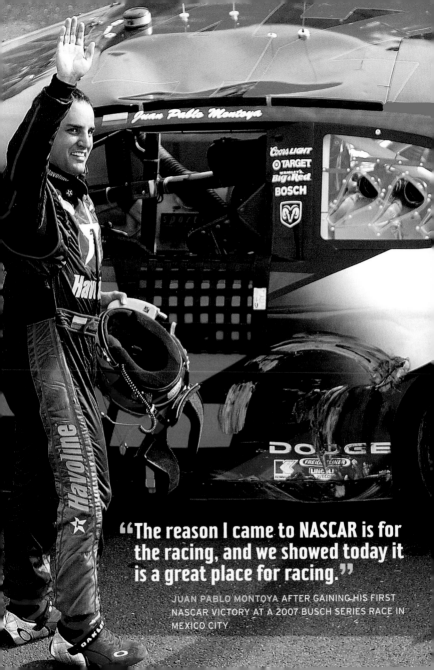

"The reason I came to NASCAR is for the racing, and we showed today it is a great place for racing."

JUAN PABLO MONTOYA AFTER GAINING HIS FIRST NASCAR VICTORY AT A 2007 BUSCH SERIES RACE IN MEXICO CITY

"Drive it like you stole it, homie."

CREW CHIEF CHAD KNAUS'S ADVICE TO JIMMIE JOHNSON
DURING THE FINAL RACE OF THE 2006 CHASE (JOHNSON HELD
ON TO FINISH NINTH AND WIN THE NEXTEL CUP CHAMPIONSHIP
BY 56 POINTS)

"There is only one lap you want to lead, and that's the last lap."

RALPH EARNHARDT, ADVISING SON DALE ON RACING

"When today's race is over, it's over. The only race that matters is the one coming up."

HARRY GANT

"No one wants to quit when he's losing and no one wants to quit when he's winning."

RICHARD PETTY

"Remember, if the world was perfect you wouldn't need roll bars in race cars."

BUDDY BAKER

"First you learn to drive fast. Next, you learn to drive fast in traffic. Then, you learn how to do it for 500 miles."

ALAN KULWICKI

"A turn is a turn. You can have all the power in the world, but if you can't get a car to corner you don't have a winner."

LEGENDARY CREW CHIEF HARRY HYDE

"Be born rich."

JANET GUTHRIE'S ADVICE ON SUCCEEDING IN RACING
(GUTHRIE WAS THE FIRST WOMAN TO DRIVE IN BOTH THE
DAYTONA 500 AND THE INDY 500 IN 1977)

"It's an emotional roller coaster ride – up and down. I've just really learned that you've got to store the highs to help you through the lows in racing."

DAVID GILLILAND, 2006 NASCAR NEWCOMER, ON WHAT HE
LEARNED IN HIS FIRST YEAR ON THE CIRCUIT

"You can't let one bad moment spoil a bunch of good ones."

DALE EARNHARDT

"The Daytona 500 is our Super Bowl. It's the one I always have been shooting for. If I had to quit racing tomorrow, I now would feel as if I had had a good racing career. "

BUDDY BAKER, WHO FINALLY WON THE DAYTONA 500 IN 1980 AFTER LEADING AT SOME POINT IN 12 OF THE PREVIOUS 13 RACES

"The great thing about the 500 being the first race of the year is it gives the teams time to prepare for our biggest race of the year. It's hard to go into the Homestead race, considering you ran at Phoenix the week before, and feel like you had adequate time to prepare for it. With our first race being the biggest one of the year, teams being able to take the time over the winter to really work on their Superspeedway cars and get ready for the Daytona 500, I think it's appropriate in all reality. I definitely don't think, because it's the biggest race of the year, you can ever put too much emphasis on it."

TONY STEWART ON THE DAYTONA 500

"In 1979, I was racing go-karts and today I had a
chance at winning the Daytona 500."

LAKE SPEED ON WHY HE WAS NOT DISAPPOINTED BY HIS
SECOND-PLACE FINISH IN THE 1985 RACE

"The Daytona 500 is one of the most storied sport-
ing events in the country and I am thrilled and
honored to be a part of it. NASCAR drivers are
tremendous athletes and I look forward to being in
that environment."

NEWLY ELECTED BASEBALL HALL OF FAMER CAL RIPKEN JR.
ON BEING CHOSEN TO DRIVE THE PACE CAR FOR THE 2007
DAYTONA 500

"I would destroy my car to win the 500 if that's
what it takes on the last lap. I don't care if the car
slid upside down across the finish line to win. This
is one of those races you'll take any chance that
you have to try to win. I won't say that's my attitude towards every race but this isn't just any race.
This is the marquee event for us this year."

TONY STEWART, WHEN ASKED HOW FAR HE WOULD GO TO
WIN THE DAYTONA 500 ON THE LAST LAP

"Growing up, racing in NASCAR late models, it's something you dream of doing. Just pulling into the racetrack for the first time and seeing the Daytona name on the wall is something I'll never forget. To be able to go race out there and learn the draft and the track, the great history behind the track, it was incredible. I definitely had butterflies."

DAVID GILLILAND, WHO WON THE POLE IN HIS FIRST TIME AT THE DAYTONA 500 IN 2007

"I've won the Daytona 500! I've won the Daytona 500! This IS Daytona, isn't it? Don't lie to me! I'm not dreaming, am I?"

DARRELL WALTRIP, WHO LEAPED OUT OF HIS CAR, DID A LITTLE DANCE AND SPIKED HIS HELMET WHEN HE WON THE 1989 DAYTONA 500, AFTER HEARTBREAKING FINISHES IN EACH OF THE PREVIOUS FOUR RACES

"I wasn't going to let anybody beat me, even if I had to block the track all the way to the checkers."

DERRIKE COPE, AFTER TAKING OVER THE LEAD ON THE FINAL TURN AT THE 1990 DAYTONA 500 AND HANGING ON FOR HIS FIRST CAREER WINSTON CUP VICTORY

"If you win the Daytona 500, you can brag all year long. You can run anywhere after the Daytona 500. If you win this thing, you won the Super Bowl."

OWNER **ROBERT YATES**

"I'm going to have minor brain surgery."

BUDDY BAKER

"Between Bobby trying to say what he was thinking and me trying to remember what he was saying, it was a helluva conversation."

NEIL BONNETT ON THE TIME BOBBY ALLISON STOPPED BY
TO SEE HIM AFTER HE'D SUFFERED TEMPORARY AMNESIA
IN A WRECK AT DARLINGTON IN 1990

"I got hit in the head pretty hard. My clock ran backwards for two years."

BUDDY BAKER

"I really don't have much of a memory of last Saturday ... I remember things like going to the driver's meeting [but] I don't remember the race, or making my first pit stop, or anything about the wreck. Really, the first thing I remember after the driver's meeting was being in the hospital. It's kind of strange how the mind works, but it's pretty much blocked out everything that happened so far."

CHAD LITTLE, AFTER SUFFERING A CONCUSSION IN A CRASH

"Well, he lived in the northern end of the house and I lived in the southern end."

WARD BURTON ON HOW HE AND BROTHER JEFF HAVE SUCH DIFFERENT ACCENTS

"Lowe's Motor Speedway is one of those tracks where the sun usually sets in the west."

MRN RADIO COMMENTATOR BARNEY HALL

"I would like to thank everybody. You know who you are and your last names."

WARD BURTON AFTER WINNING AT LOUDEN IN NEW HAMPSHIRE

"I said if we don't come and they come, they're going to beat us. If we do come and they come we'll win and if we do come and they don't come we'll win, so I said we have to come in."

CARL EDWARDS, WHOSE DECISION TO COME INTO THE PIT FOR FOUR NEW TIRES NEARLY COST HIM THE 2005 3M PERFORMANCE 400

"I could stand up in the seat and not hit my head."

BUDDY BAKER ON THE SIZE OF ONE OF HIS OLD PLYMOUTHS

"I ain't as big as I once was, but I was good once as I
  ever was."

MICHAEL WALTRIP, ON LEARNING THAT THE POLE POSI-
TION HE EARNED FOR THE 2005 POCONO 500 WAS THE
FIRST TIME TIME HE'D BEEN ON THE POLE SINCE 1991

"Why can't I just not say never?
You'll see when I don't show up there."

MARK MARTIN WHO PLANNED TO RACE ONLY PART-TIME IN
2007, BUT WAS REPEATEDLY ASKED IF HE'D RECONSIDER
AFTER TAKING THE POINTS LEAD EARLY IN THE SEASON

"If I have a love-hate relationship with Martinsville,
  then we're missing the love part of the equation."

TONY STEWART

"I get up to speed pretty easy."

JUAN PABLO MONTOYA ON THE TRANSITION FROM OPEN
WHEEL TO STOCK CAR RACING AS HE PREPARED TO
BECOME THE FIRST DRIVER TO LEAVE FORMULA ONE
FOR NASCAR

"We've got heavy hearts in the backs of our minds."

KURT BUSCH, EXPRESSING HIS FEELINGS ON OWNER JACK
ROUSH IN THE AFTERMATH OF ROUSH'S INJURIES IN A
PLANE CRASH

"Driving that car, I felt like I was sitting on a pickle bucket."

MICHAEL WALTRIP, COMMENTING ON THE SEATING
POSITION IN A BOUGHT RIDE LATE IN THE 2006 SEASON,
AFTER HIS TEAM FAILED TO MAKE THE RACE

"I've always said your legacy is what you leave behind you."

DARRELL WALTRIP

"Martinsville is the kind of track that you either love or hate, and I've learned to do both."

KURT BUSCH, AFTER WINNING THE POLE FOR THE 2006
SUBWAY 500 AT MARTINSVILLE SPEEDWAY

"A man must want money awful bad to drive there."

RICHARD PETTY, WHO REFUSED TO DRIVE AT INDIANAPOLIS

"They look like cucumbers with hayraker wheels."

JOE WEATHERLY, NASCAR LEGEND OF THE 1950s AND 60s,
ON HIS DISDAIN FOR INDY CARS OF THE ERA

"I've learned to never say never, but I look at my life as a book and it's kind of like it's a chapter that's either on its last page or almost closed. My contract takes me to 39 and I don't see myself getting back into Indy Car at the age of 39."

FORMER INDY CAR DRIVER AND TWO-TIME NASCAR
CHAMPION TONY STEWART WHEN ASKED PRIOR TO
THE 2007 NASCAR SEASON IF HE MIGHT EVER RACE IN
THE INDIANAPOLIS 500 AGAIN

"If you would bring an engineer from Formula One and show them how detailed the cars are, they would be shocked."

JUAN PABLO MONTOYA, WHILE PREPARING TO BECOME
THE FIRST DRIVER TO LEAVE FORMULA ONE FOR NASCAR

"I've had a jackass driving for me, and now I am rid
of him."

JUNIOR JOHNSON, COMMENTING ON DARRELL WALTRIP'S
SWITCH TO HENDRICKS AFTER THE 1986 SEASON

"I was like a pig with a wristwatch."

BUDDY BAKER ON THE GIBSON GUITAR HE WON AT
NASHVILLE

"He's got a 10-foot ego, and a 4-foot body, and it ain't working too good right now."

MIKE BLISS, AFTER BOBBY HAMILTON JR. KNOCKED HIM
OUT OF THE 2003 NEW ENGLAND 200

"That's the problem with him. Nobody has ever
really grabbed him and given him a good beating."

NASCAR CAR OWNER **RAY EVERNHAM** ON TONY STEWART,
AFTER STEWART SPUN OUT EVERNHAM'S DRIVER KASEY
KAHNE IN THE 2004 TROPICANA 400 AT CHICAGOLAND
SPEEDWAY

"The problem is you've got a young kid who is trying to replace Dale Earnhardt, who thinks he is Dale Earnhardt, and right now he wouldn't be a scab on Dale Earnhardt's butt."

BOBBY HAMILTON ON THEN-ROOKIE KEVIN HARVICK

"I couldn't hear him. He's got that little yap-yap mouth. I couldn't tell what he was saying."

RICKY RUDD, WHEN ASKED WHAT KEVIN HARVICK SAID TO HIM AFTER RUDD SPUN HIM INTO THE WALL WITH EIGHT LAPS REMAINING IN THE 2003 CHEVY ROCK AND ROLL 400 AT RICHMOND

"I gotta thank Ron Hornaday – for continuing to prove that he is the most disrespectful driver on the racetrack."

SCOTT RIGGS, AFTER BEING RUN INTO THE WALL BY HORNADAY ON A RESTART LATE IN THE 2003 FUNAI 250 AT RICHMOND

"Everybody else got by us, but that cue-ball-headed fool can't get by us without wrecking us."

DALE EARNHARDT JR. ON TODD BODINE

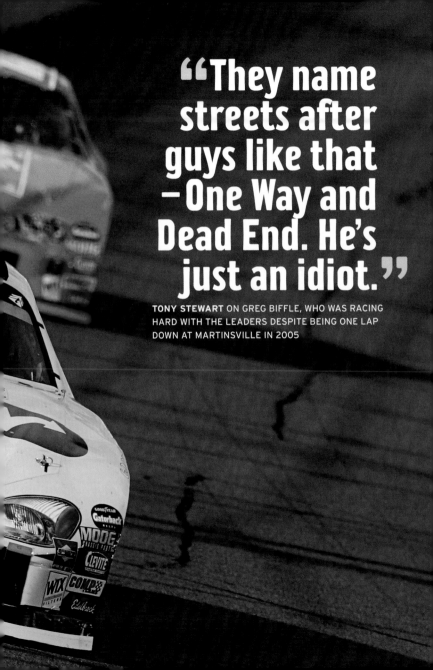

"They name streets after guys like that – One Way and Dead End. He's just an idiot."

TONY STEWART ON GREG BIFFLE, WHO WAS RACING HARD WITH THE LEADERS DESPITE BEING ONE LAP DOWN AT MARTINSVILLE IN 2005

"He ran out of talent about halfway through the corner."

BUDDY BAKER ON A DRIVER IN A PRO TRUCK RACE

"I got run over by the bug-eyed dummy, I guess."

STERLING MARLIN, WHO HAD APPEARED TO GIVE GREG BIFFLE SOME ROOM, AFTER BIFFLE SPUN HIM INTO THE WALL AT WATKINS GLEN IN 2004

"I don't know if any of you have seen Kurt's arms, but I've seen bigger muscles on a squirrel's leg."

MICHAEL WALTRIP ON KURT BUSCH

"It's his life, not mine. I'm sure if James Hylton could do it, I could. But I've got better sense."

JUNIOR JOHNSON ON 72-YEAR-OLD HYLTON'S ATTEMPT TO MAKE THE 2007 DAYTONA 500 FIELD (HIS LAST RACE HAD BEEN IN 1993)

"I hope my boys make good in racing cause they'll starve to death if they don't."

GEORGE ELLIOTT, FATHER OF BILL, ERNIE AND DAN

"You've got three kinds of drivers. Over here is
  Earnhardt. Then you've got two or three others
  who can run with him. Then there's the rest."

VETERAN CAR OWNER BUD MOORE

"You go back to the start of time. One cave guy was
  fighting another cave guy because his club was
  bigger than his or his woman had longer hair.
  That's competition."

DALE EARNHARDT

"Finishing races is important, but racing is more important."

DALE EARNHARDT

"I got in the ambulance and looked back over there
  and I said, 'Man, the wheels ain't knocked off that
  car yet. Get out. I gotta go.'"

DALE EARNHARDT AFTER A WRECK IN 1997

"I've got to win every race."

DALE EARNHARDT

"The winner ain't the one with the fastest car, it's the one who refuses to lose."

DALE EARNHARDT

"It's a never-ending battle of making your cars better and also trying to be better yourself."

DALE EARNHARDT

"When he was young, I told Dale Jr. that hunting and racing are a lot alike. Holding that steering wheel and holding that rifle both mean you better be responsible."

DALE EARNHARDT

"You've got to be closer to the edge than ever to win. That means sometimes you go over the edge, and I don't mean driving, either."

DALE EARNHARDT

"I guess he lives up to that commercial where he plays the Tasmanian devil. His wild side comes out."

BOBBY LABONTE ON DALE EARNHARDT

"Most people saw him as intimidating, but really it was his level of confidence in himself. He had that confidence that nobody could beat him. His confidence level is what gave him that edge."

CREW CHIEF ANDY PETREE ON DALE EARNHARDT

"When I came into Winston Cup, I didn't have nothing."

DALE EARNHARDT

"You've got to have and use every resource that you have to win."

DALE EARNHARDT

"I never went into racing to be a bad guy, a good guy, any guy, just a good racer. I wanted to be Dale Earnhardt the racer. We've won races and championships not because I'm a good guy or a bad guy. I'm a good racer. I've got a good race team and we are out there to win."

DALE EARNHARDT, PLAYING DOWN HIS MAN IN BLACK, INTIMIDATOR IMAGE

"I haven't really thought about it. The only thing I worry about is winning ... races and the championship. It's like hunting and fishing. You want to catch the most fish or shoot the most ducks – with the least shells. You don't want to be standing there with a whole pile of shells on the ground and one duck."

DALE EARNHARDT, WHEN ASKED WHERE HE THOUGHT HE RANKED AMONG THE GREATEST DRIVERS OF ALL TIME

"When you beat Dale Earnhardt anywhere at anything, any time, you know you've had a day's work."

DALE JARRETT AFTER BEATING DALE EARNHARDT TO WIN THE 1993 DAYTONA 500

"Trying to keep him behind me is one of the hardest things I've ever done at Daytona."

JEFF GORDON ON HOLDING OFF DALE EARNHARDT IN THE FINAL LAPS TO WIN THE 1999 DAYTONA 500

"All I have to say is I hope they give me this ride next year for the entire season. I think I can be tough. If some people didn't know before, they know now I can drive a race car."

DALE EARNHARDT AFTER HIS FIRST RACE FOR OWNER ROD OSTERLUND IN THE SECOND LAST RACE OF THE 1979 SEASON

"That just beats all I've ever seen. If there was ever a perfect race car, that was it. I'm a disappointed man right now."

BUDDY BAKER, WHO WON THE POLE WITH A RECORD SPEED OF 196.049 MPH AT THE 1979 DAYTONA 500, ONLY TO PULL OUT AFTER 38 LAPS DUE TO IGNITION PROBLEMS

"What a heartbreaker. To be a half mile from something you've dreamed about all your life – man, that's awfully hard to take."

OWNER RICHARD CHILDRESS, WHEN TIRE TROUBLES ON THE LAST LAP COST DALE EARNHARDT THE 1990 DAYTONA 500 AFTER LEADING THROUGH 155 OF 200 LAPS

"I'm not supposed to win the damn thing, I don't reckon."

DALE EARNHARDT, AFTER FINISHING SECOND AT THE 1995 DAYTONA 500

"I'm still happy every time I get a chance to come to Victory Lane here at Daytona, but obviously I'd trade all three of these Shootouts and both Pepsi 400s to win one Daytona 500."

TONY STEWART

"At least we know we can win there in July."

"We've definitely figured out how to win Saturday night races here at Daytona. We've just got to figure out how to win a Sunday race."

"I didn't ask for a win in the Daytona 500, I asked for a chance."

"I had a horror of kissing girls before a race. It started many years ago when I was a rookie. A girl kissed me before a race and I spun out and backed through a fence. She kissed me later and the same thing happened. In an effort to break the jinx, she kissed me twice before the next race. So what happens? I flip end over end seven times. I don't even kiss my wife before a race."

GLENN "FIREBALL" ROBERTS, WHO FINALLY WON THE DAYTONA 500 IN 1962 DESPITE THE FACT THAT FORMER MISS AMERICA MARY ANN MOBLEY HAD GIVEN THE SUPER-STITIOUS DRIVER A KISS FOR LUCK BEFORE THE RACE

"I kept waiting for Fireball to blow up."

RICHARD PETTY AFTER FINISHING SECOND TO GLENN "FIREBALL" ROBERTS AT THE 1962 DAYTONA 500

"Son, I'm just **too mad** to write today."

GLENN "FIREBALL" ROBERTS, TO A YOUNG AUTOGRAPH HOUND AFTER A FLUKE MISHAP KNOCKED HIM OUT OF THE 1961 DAYTONA 500, WHICH HE HAD BEEN LEADING FOR 170 OF THE FIRST 187 LAPS. BAD LUCK HAD ALSO COST HIM VICTORIES AT DAYTONA IN 1959 AND 1960

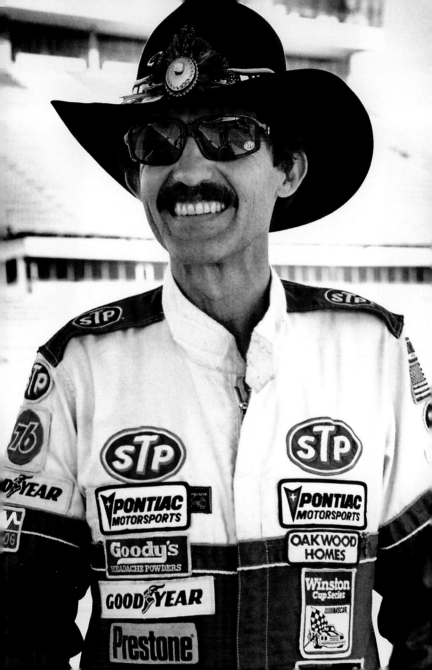

"You've got to have a lead dog. You've got to have somebody out there for everybody to shoot at."

RICHARD PETTY, WHOSE 200 CAREER VICTORIES, INCLUDING SEVEN WINS AT THE DAYTONA 500, ARE BY FAR THE MOST IN NASCAR HISTORY

"We never went to a race we didn't think we could win. We thought we were supposed to."

2007 NATIONAL MOTORSPORTS PRESS ASSOCIATION HALL OF FAME INDUCTEE MAURICE PETTY, BROTHER OF RICHARD PETTY AND ACE ENGINE BUILDER ON HIS CREW

"Racing is where you run up there and beat on someone, and you get by them and then you go on to the next guy."

RICHARD PETTY

"I probably run harder when I'm in 10th place than I do when I'm leading ... because I don't like to be in 10th place, and I do everything I can to improve my situation."

RICHARD PETTY

"I ran harder here today than I ever have in my whole life. I was almost flat out all the way. At first I wasn't sure I could beat everybody, but as the race went along, I was pretty confident I could."

RICHARD PETTY, RETURNING IN 1966 TO WIN THE DAYTONA 500 (WHICH HE HAD ALSO WON IN 1964) AFTER SITTING OUT A YEAR BECAUSE OF NASCAR'S BAN ON CHRYSLER'S HEMI ENGINE

"The big deal I remember about that race, we were coming off the number-four corner down the straightaway and Joe Weatherly blew a tire and went right through the grandstand fence. There were boards and things flying everywhere and I put my hands up over my face. It was just an automatic thing, and when I realized I'd taken my hands off the steering wheel I couldn't believe it and it like to have scared me to death. I said, 'Man, I can't be doing this!' But I just kept on doin' it."

RICHARD PETTY, RECALLING HIS FIRST NASCAR RACE

"I think all them cats wanted was an autograph because none of them brought a fire extinguisher.
I had to holler at them to bring one. "

RICHARD PETTY, WHO DROVE DOWN TO THE FIRST TURN WHERE THE FIRE TRUCKS WERE WHEN HIS CAR CAUGHT FIRE IN A CRASH IN THE FINAL RACE OF HIS CAREER AT THE 1992 HOOTERS 500 AT ATLANTA

"When you talk to me, you're talking to history. I've seen all the changes. Some of them were good and some were bad. No matter what NASCAR throws at us, we cope with it."

RICHARD PETTY ON THE MANY CHANGES NASCAR INTRODUCED FOR THE 2007 SEASON

"I had Beauchamp by a good two feet. In my own mind, I know I won."

LEE PETTY, WHOSE TIGHT WIN OVER JOHNNY BEAUCHAMP AT THE FIRST DAYTONA 500 IN 1959 HAD TO BE CONFIRMED BY INSTANT REPLAY

"I'd win the race! If I had it to do over again, I'd have hit David harder."

RICHARD PETTY, WHO LOST THE 1976 DAYTONA 500 WHEN DAVID PEARSON RESTARTED HIS CAR FIRST AFTER THEIR COLLISION, WHEN ASKED WHAT HE'D DO DIFFERENTLY IF HE COULD RUN THE LAST LAP OVER AGAIN

"This victory is sweeter than the one in 1985. Then, the car was superior. Today, it was only equal to some others and I had to race it. This was the kind of race that keeps you pumped because it was so close. You have to beat the competition in every way, on the track and on the pits."

BILL ELLIOTT ON HIS 1987 DAYTONA 500 VICTORY

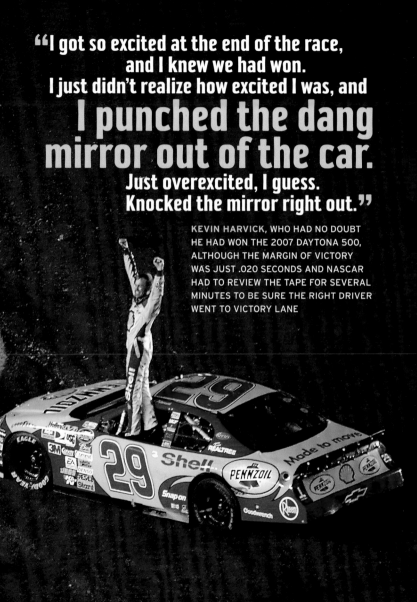

"I got so excited at the end of the race, and I knew we had won. I just didn't realize how excited I was, and **I punched the dang mirror out of the car.** Just overexcited, I guess. Knocked the mirror right out."

KEVIN HARVICK, WHO HAD NO DOUBT HE HAD WON THE 2007 DAYTONA 500, ALTHOUGH THE MARGIN OF VICTORY WAS JUST .020 SECONDS AND NASCAR HAD TO REVIEW THE TAPE FOR SEVERAL MINUTES TO BE SURE THE RIGHT DRIVER WENT TO VICTORY LANE

"Any time you beat Dale Earnhardt in one of those late-race deals, it's real special. But if Earnhardt or anybody else had been in my car, they would have won. That's how good it was."

STERLING MARLIN, AFTER HOLDING OFF DALE EARNHARDT TO WIN HIS SECOND CONSECUTIVE DAYTONA 500 IN 1995

"The last lap was close to 500 miles itself. I'd rather look in the mirror and see anybody but that 3 car back there."

DALE JARRETT, AFTER HOLDING OFF DALE EARNHARDT TO WIN THE 1996 DAYTONA 500

"It was an awesome race. I didn't give him room in [Turn] one and he didn't give me room in [Turn] four. That's the way it's supposed to be. This was simple great hard racing."

KURT BUSCH ON THE 2003 CAROLINA DODGE DEALERS 400, WHERE HE LOST HIS POWER STEERING WITH 10 LAPS TO GO, AND THEN TRADED SHEET METAL WITH RICKY CRAVEN DOWN THE FINAL STRAIGHTAWAY, ONLY TO LOSE BY 0.002 OF A SECOND IN THE CLOSEST FINISH SINCE NASCAR ADOPTED ELECTRONIC SCORING IN 1993

"Richard, if you expect to make it in anything, you have to try a little bit harder than the rest. I don't care if you're a clown in a circus or trying to sell pots and pans, you have to work harder than the next man if you want to be the best."

ADVICE FROM LEE PETTY TO HIS SON RICHARD

"Expect to work long hours for very little or no pay. Pay attention to what the fast cars are doing. Keep good records, both setups and financial. Be clean. This includes you, your crew, transporter, car, tools and pit equipment. Also, send flowers to your wife or girlfriend often. It never hurts!"

ADVICE FROM ARCA [AUTOMOBILE RACING CLUB ASSOCIATION] CHAMPION FRANK KIMMEL

"You have to go on instincts for one thing – and hope that your instincts are right. I think after you make enough mistakes, you learn when they're right and when they're wrong."

DAVEY ALLISON

"I'm just a guy from Kannapolis, North Carolina,
a cotton-mill town, made it to the eighth grade in
school. I went out there and did what I could do
and excelled at what I could do."

DALE EARNHARDT

"Not yet. When I'm gone I'll be a legend. Right now,
I'm just very good at what I do."

DICK TRICKLE

"I didn't have any."

NASCAR LEGEND CURTIS TURNER REPLYING TO THE
QUESTION "WHO WAS YOUR TOUGHEST COMPETITION
OUT THERE?" AFTER A BLOWN ENGINE KNOCKED HIM
OUT OF THE RACE WHILE LEADING AT DAYTONA

"What makes the Monte Carlo so good? Me!"

DALE EARNHARDT

"You can take 10 of us who ran back in the 1950s and 60s, put all the winnings together, and Dale Jarrett won more than that in the 2000 Daytona 500."

COTTON OWENS

"I enjoyed every minute of it. Didn't make a whole lot of money, but if I could do it again today, I'd do it. And I think I'd make it."

LOUISE SMITH, THE FIRST WOMAN DRIVER IN NASCAR (IN THE 1940s AND 1950s)

"Pay my damn debts."

TINY LUND'S ANSWER, WHEN ASKED WHAT HE PLANNED TO DO WITH ALL THAT MONEY AFTER GETTING HIS FIRST CAREER WIN AT THE 1963 DAYTONA 500

"Charlotte. Because it pays the most."

DAVID PEARSON, WHEN ASKED (IN 1965) WHICH RACE HE'D PREFER TO WIN

"We drove for the sheer fun of driving because there wasn't that much money to be made."

RICHARD PETTY ON HIS EARLY DAYS IN NASCAR

"Sometimes it seemed like **the more you drove the less money you had.** I remember one time Buck Baker and Lee Petty and I **had to put our money together just to split a hot dog and a Coke."**

LOUISE SMITH, THE FIRST WOMAN DRIVER IN NASCAR (IN THE 1940s AND 1950s)

"The money falls out of the sky to these people now – the drivers and even the crew chiefs. Back then, a year fifth in points making $40,000 in a total year, well that was actually a pretty decent year."

ELMO LANGLEY, WHO DROVE THE WINSTON CUP
SERIES PACE CAR DURING THE 1990s, BUT HAD BEEN
A RACER BACK IN THE 1950s

"It's amazing, isn't it? Who would have ever thought it would get to this point? As a matter of a fact, me and some of the other older guys are really jealous – because they pay real money now. It's come a long way."

MARVIN PANCH, 1961 DAYTONA 500 WINNER,
ON NASCAR TODAY

"When I first started racing I never dreamt – never dreamt! – that you could make the kind of money that I'm making for driving a race car. And I would drive for free."

JIMMY SPENCER

"Well, I don't know which one has more money, but I'll tell you what. Either one could burn a wet mule with hundred-dollar bills."

BUDDY BAKER ON OWNERS RICK HENDRICK AND FELIX SABATES

"Can't believe it. Unbelievable. But it's a different era. Everything in the world has changed. I'm just glad I put my money away."

FRED LORENZEN, NASCAR LEGEND WHO RETIRED IN 1967 AT AGE 33, ON THE RICHES IN RACING TODAY

"We're making lots of money. But other than a Dale Jr., Jeff Gordon or Tony Stewart, I don't think anyone in NASCAR is making the type of money like [the New York Yankees'] Derek Jeter or Alex Rodriguez."

KASEY KAHNE

"We have to do good. It's not a situation where we have long-term contracts. We want to win races and win poles as fastest qualifiers."

JOE NEMECHEK

"Those boys playing football get their two or three million dollars up front, and if they don't have a good day, they are not out anything. They still get paid on Monday. If we don't win, we don't get paid on Monday."

RICHARD PETTY

"The doctor just told me that the first time I came back it was a full-fledged miracle. He kind of explained to me how many miracles you can have. That kind of woke me up."

ERNIE IRVAN ANNOUNCING HIS RETIREMENT

"I remember when I regained consciousness, I asked the doctor if I could race that next week."

GEOFFREY BODINE, WHO WAS LUCKY TO SURVIVE A CRASH AT DAYTONA IN THE INAUGURAL NASCAR CRAFTSMAN TRUCK SERIES IN 2000

"I realized I better enjoy and appreciate and con- tribute as much as I can today because all of this could be gone tomorrow."

DAVEY ALLISON, AFTER WATCHING REPLAYS OF HIS HORRIFYING 1992 POCONO CRASH

"There's no good explanation why one wreck hurts somebody and another doesn't. When it's your turn, it's your time. That's how I have to live or I'd have 20 ulcers."

BUFFY WALTRIP, WIFE OF MICHAEL WALTRIP

"The Lord works miracles. He did one yesterday in front of 35,000 people."

MICHAEL WALTRIP FOLLOWING HIS HORRIFIC CRASH IN
1990 AT BRISTOL

"The one thing that you'll never change is when you crash one of those, you hit escape and you start over. I've tried that a couple times so far in a Cup car. You don't get a chance to restart, and the team really lets you know about that."

A.J. ALLMENDINGER ON NASCAR VIDEO GAMES

"We were racing along and someone must have got into me, because next thing I knew, I seen the people up there in the back straightaway, in the bleachers, up there eating chicken. You can't pay two dollars at the state fair to ride something like that."

CARL LONG, WHO WAS BUMPED BY JOE NEMECHEK ON LAP
263 AT THE 2004 SUBWAY 400. HIS CAR TURNED ON ITS SIDE
AS IT SKIDDED ALONG THE TRACK, THEN BARREL-ROLLED
SEVERAL TIMES BEFORE FINALLY COMING TO A STOP

"The crashes people remember, but drivers remember the near misses."

MARIO ANDRETTI

"That was one of the hardest hits I've ever taken. One of the worst things you can ever ask for is the brakes to go out in Turn one of Pocono."

JEFF GORDON, AFTER HITTING THE WALL WHEN HIS BRAKES
FAILED WITH 10 LAPS TO GO AT THE 2006 POCONO 500

"I feel like I could run another 500-mile race right now and still feel the same. I felt good all day in the car, but I'm sure when the adrenaline wears off, I'm going to be sore."

TONY STEWART, AFTER DRIVING ALL 500 MILES AT THE
2006 POCONO 500 JUST TWO WEEKS AFTER BREAKING HIS
RIGHT SHOULDER BLADE

"It was a good run for Bobby. It is awful tough to race with a broken scapula. I know because I have done it before. But, I didn't do it one week after I broke it."

TERRY LABONTE ON BROTHER BOBBY, WHO FINISHED
THIRD AT A 1999 RACE AT THE TEXAS MOTOR SPEEDWAY
(WON BY TERRY) JUST NINE DAYS AFTER BREAKING HIS
RIGHT SHOULDER

"It's OK but it sure hurt there for awhile. I guess these old bones ain't as young as they used to be."

RICHARD PETTY, AFTER DISLOCATING HIS SHOULDER
WHEN HIS CAR SLAMMED HARD INTO THE SECOND TURN
WALL ON THE 66TH LAP OF THE 1986 DAYTONA 500

**"That's the biggest problem
that we have today.
There's only so much that you
can do about it in there,
and you have to understand going
into it how hot it's going to be.
On a very hot day, when we get
into the middle of summer,
you're going to get
temperatures of 125 to 130
degrees in there – and that's
just the temperature
inside the car.
The floor pans
get a lot hotter than that."**

DALE JARRETT ON THE HEAT INSIDE MODERN CARS

"We fear flame, but it is the heat that can be dangerous. The flame is visible, but the heat burns you and it's still there after the flame is gone. It's like a campfire. You sit too close to the campfire and you can feel the heat on your face, and you back away. When you're in a race car and it's 750 degrees, you're basically in an oven."

CHAD LIBERTO, DIRECTOR OF TEAM SALES AND RACING SERVICES FOR SPARCO USA

"It's really hot shut up in there. It's so hot the floor burns your feet."

ROCKY MORAN ON WHAT IT'S LIKE IN THE CAR

"Most race drivers are very impatient. They won't wait for things to happen. They've got to make them happen. Nine out of ten do their racing at the beginning of the race, but I do mine at the end. In a 500-mile race, you run the first 490 miles for exercise."

RICHARD PETTY

"You have to drive 400 miles at a pace that you feel the car will be comfortable at and you're comfortable at and you can finish at. The last 100 miles you can do what you need to win the race. It's so hard to learn that."

JIMMY SPENCER, WHO CREDITS TRAVIS CARTER WITH HELPING HIM TO LEARN TO CURB HIS TENDENCY TO RACE ALL-OUT ALL THE TIME

"I made so many mistakes in being aggressive that I either crashed or won. I never got second or third or fourth. I either got last or I won. That was being too aggressive and taking too many chances. The moral of the story is don't try too hard. Second, third or fourth is OK. It doesn't have to be a victory every time, and sometimes you have a fifth-place car."

GREG BIFFLE

> **"The hardest part of being patient is knowing that you want to move up, but you don't have an opportunity to — and accepting it."**

DAVEY ALLISON

"I think the biggest thing in the video games, you learn patience. Because in the video games – you can get in trouble a lot quicker than you can on the racetrack."

MIKE FORD, CREW CHIEF FOR DENNY HAMLIN, WHO IS AMONG SEVERAL NASCAR DRIVERS WHO PARTICIPATE IN SIMULATED RACING

"That's how you win races. If you can stay in there, you can figure on some of 'em falling out for one thing or another. My car was probably the seventh-fastest here, but it was first across the line."

RICHARD PETTY, WHO OUTSMARTED, OUTLUCKED AND OUTLASTED HIS MAIN RIVALS TO WIN HIS SEVENTH DAYTONA 500 IN 1981

"You want to be in the top five, racing for the lead."

DALE EARNHARDT

"Why would you race if you weren't going to be up front?"

DICK TRICKLE

"I never lost my job while I was leading a race."

BUDDY BAKER

"If you run as hard as you can in every race, good things will happen for you."

JEFF GORDON

"I drove flat out. I never looked nowhere but straight ahead."

STERLING MARLIN, WHOSE VICTORY AT THE 1994 DAYTONA 500 WAS THE FIRST VICTORY BY EITHER HIM OR HIS FATHER COO COO AFTER 443 WINSTON CUP RACES

"He played 'catch me if you can' and nobody could."

BOBBY ALLISON ON THE FAST PACE SET BY BILL ELLIOTT EN ROUTE TO WINNING THE 1985 DAYTONA 500

"My purpose in life was to run 100 percent. Maybe it cost me some races, but nobody ever hired me to ride."

BUDDY BAKER

"Nobody remembers who finished second but the guy who finished second."

BOBBY UNSER

"I'm going to run the hell out of 'em every lap. I've never won a race stroking."

GLENN "FIREBALL" ROBERTS

"I ran out of brains with about five to go and hit the wall a couple of times. I just saw Kurt [Busch] and wanted to win so bad. I'd rather mess up trying."

MICHAEL WALTRIP AT THE 2005 SUBWAY FRESH 500 AT THE PHOENIX INTERNATIONAL RACEWAY

"Second place is just the first loser."

DALE EARNHARDT

"Basically, my philosophy is to keep working and try. It'll all eventually work out. If it doesn't, so what? You've got be doing something anyhow. "

DAVE MARCIS

"I got most of my advice from my dad. He told me so dadgum much. I guess probably as much as anything he said, 'Be fair with people. Cut through all the stuff.' "

RICHARD PETTY ON THE BEST ADVICE HE EVER RECEIVED

"Success is being happy with yourself."

KYLE PETTY

"Tough times are the Lord's way of teaching me to be strong."

GEOFFREY BODINE

"Racing is a matter of spirit not strength."

JANET GUTHRIE, THE FIRST WOMAN TO DRIVE IN BOTH THE DAYTONA 500 AND THE INDY 500 IN 1977

"The pressure is immense — no other way to say it. There is so much effort and money put into the program that you never want to let down your teammates and sponsors. Never."

JOE NEMECHEK

"When I won my first race, it was the ultimate feeling at that point. But two days from then you wake up and you're like, 'All right. I've got to do it again.' This is similar to that. It's been a great off-season, but you've got to do it again."

JIMMIE JOHNSON ON THE PRESSURE TO REPEAT AFTER WINNING HIS FIRST NEXTEL CUP CHAMPIONSHIP IN 2006

"Nobody puts more pressure on me to perform than myself. I know when I get out of the car if I gave 100 percent. I'm very honest with myself and I know the team is, too."

JIMMIE JOHNSON

"These guys aren't having fun anymore ... They have a lot of pressure on them. They have to perform, and they have a lot of people they have to beat. When I was running, we had just a few people that we had to beat. You could have a bad day and still finish sixth or seventh. Now, if you are off a little bit, you finish 37th."

DARRELL WALTRIP

"After nine laps at Dover several years ago, Ken Schrader got hit from behind and spun out. I had to go back to the garage and interview him. The team was working on the bent-up race car so I asked him, 'Kenny, can you get back out on the track?' And he said, 'Yeah, I'm afraid so.'"

PIT REPORTER STEVE BYRNES

"We had the wrong gear, wrong springs, wrong shocks and wrong car. We had the right beer, but other than that, we got stomped."

STERLING MARLIN (WHO IS SPONSORED BY COORS LITE)

"We're having chassis, aero and motor problems. Other than that, things are great."

WARD BURTON

"Why did I take up racing? I was too lazy to work and too chicken to steal."

KYLE PETTY

"It's basically the same, just darker."

ALAN KULWICKI, WHEN ASKED TO COMPARE NIGHT RACING
TO DAYTIME RACING

"I'll apologize to them after they get me to the front!"

DALE EARNHARDT ON BEING TOLD BY HIS CREW CHIEF
THAT HE WAS HURTING HIS TIRES AND NEEDED TO
CONSERVE THEM

"You drive the car, you don't carry it."

JANET GUTHRIE, THE FIRST WOMAN TO DRIVE IN BOTH THE
DAYTONA 500 AND THE INDY 500, WHEN ASKED IF SHE HAD
THE STRENGTH TO RACE CARS

"DEI without Dale Earnhardt Jr. is a museum."

TONY STEWART ON THE POSSIBILITY OF JUNIOR LEAVING
DALE EARNHARDT INC.

"If I dig any deeper, I'll be in China."

KYLE BUSCH, WHEN TOLD BY HIS TEAM TO "DIG IN"
DURING THE LATTER STAGES OF THE 2006 NEIGHBORHOOD
EXCELLENCE 400 AT DOVER INTERNATIONAL SPEEDWAY.
HE FINISHED FIFTH

"Well, this is the only thing I won this year."

BILL ELLIOTT ON BEING VOTED THE MOST POPULAR
DRIVER OF 1996, THE 11TH TIME HE WON THE AWARD

"Understeer is hitting the wall with the front of your car. Oversteer is hitting it with the rear."

GLENN "FIREBALL" ROBERTS

"We go six times faster."

NASCAR CEO WILLIAM C. FRANCE, WHEN ASKED WHY
DEATHS IN AUTO RACING WERE SIX TIMES MORE COMMON
THAN DEATHS IN FOOTBALL

"In what other sport do you get a 15-second break every hour?"

DALE EARNHARDT ON THE QUESTION OF WHETHER
DRIVERS ARE ATHLETES

"I told Kasey if he wanted a hot dog, we would have just bought him one."

TEAM OWNER RAY EVERNHAM AFTER KASEY KAHNE WON
THE 2006 3M PEFORMANCE 400 DESPITE HAVING TO PULL
INTO THE PIT AFTER RUNNING INTO DEBRIS (INCLUDING
HOT DOG WRAPPERS) THAT HAD BLOWN ONTO THE TRACK

"The new asphalt is like putting a tuxedo on a rattlesnake."

BUDDY BAKER ON THE RE-PAVED DARLINGTON RACETRACK

"I came to a race and a rodeo broke out. That's all I've got to say."

JIMMY SPENCER'S THOUGHTS ON QUALIFYING LAPS AT DAYTONA

"That's one question I'll never have to worry about."

RICHARD PETTY, 1973 DAYTONA 500 CHAMP, WHEN ASKED IF HE COULD HAVE HELD OFF BUDDY BAKER (BAKER WAS CLOSING FAST WHEN HIS ENGINE EXPLODED WITH SIX LAPS TO GO)

"I didn't have time to be angry. If he had beat me across the line, I might have been."

DAVID PEARSON, AFTER BEATING RICHARD PETTY BY RESTARTING HIS CAR FIRST, FOLLOWING THEIR LAST-LAP CRASH IN A WILD FINISH AT THE 1976 DAYTONA 500

"I'm about 15 pounds heavier. I've got highlights in my hair."

TONY STEWART ON WHAT HAS CHANGED SINCE HIS 2002 WINSTON CUP CHAMPIONSHIP

"When I saw the wall coming through the car, I knew I was in trouble."

MIKE HARMON, AFTER WALKING AWAY FROM A GRUESOME CRASH DURING A BUSCH GRAND NATIONAL PRACTICE SESSION AT BRISTOL

"When I started out on asphalt and wound up on dirt, I knew I was in trouble."

JIMMY HORTON, AFTER GOING OVER THE WALL AND ONTO A DIRT LANE OUTSIDE AND WELL BELOW THE TRACK, AT TALLADEGA IN 1993

"You can tell that you're in trouble when you feel the air on the back of your neck instead of in your face."

BUDDY BAKER

"Fairly or not, [NASCAR] racing is more closely identified with the lore, legends and legacy of the Old South than any other sport except, possibly, professional bass fishing. Our leading commentator on things Southern, North Carolina sociologist John Shelton Reed, includes entries on stock car racing, Junior Johnson, Richard Petty and the Darlington Speedway in *1001 Things Everyone Should Know About the South.*"

WRITER JIM WRIGHT IN HIS BOOK "FIXIN' TO GIT: ONE FAN'S LOVE AFFAIR WITH NASCAR'S WINSTON CUP"

"Certainly the vivid display of Confederate battle flags at [NASCAR] events adds to the impression that stock car racing is (or was until Jeff Gordon came along) a Southern sport contested mainly by Southern drivers and enjoyed mainly by Southern fans."

WRITER JIM WRIGHT ON THE STEREOTYPE THAT NASCAR IS THE QUINTESSENTIAL SOUTHERN SPORT

"Two of my favorite things are my steering wheel and my Remington rifle."

DALE EARNHARDT

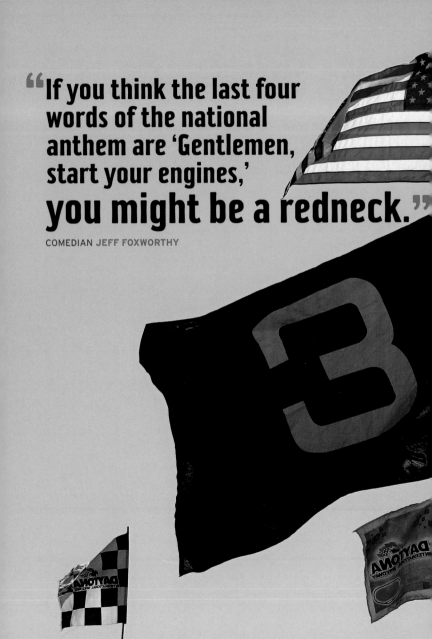

"If you think the last four words of the national anthem are 'Gentlemen, start your engines,' you might be a redneck."

COMEDIAN JEFF FOXWORTHY

"Like all stereotypes, this one has a substantial basis in fact. NASCAR's first non-Southern champion, Bill Rexford of New York, was crowned in 1950, in NASCAR's second season. The second non-Southern champion, Alan Kulwicki of Wisconsin, wasn't crowned until 1992. So Southern drivers have literally dominated the competition over the years."

WRITER JIM WRIGHT ON THE STEREOTYPE THAT NASCAR IS THE QUINTESSENTIAL SOUTHERN SPORT

"NASCAR has changed so much in the last five years because you don't have as many of the good old Southern boys as you used to. Jeff Gordon or Jimmie Johnson or myself come from the west coast and so many different racing series. It's a matter of the best drivers want to come to NASCAR to show their talents and its more accepted that an Indy Car guy can come here and give it a shot. So I'm thankful for that and I know a lot of the other drivers are, too. We just want to prove ourselves on the racetrack."

J.J. YELEY, WHEN ASKED IF HE FELT PEOPLE ARE NOW MORE ACCEPTING OF NASCAR DRIVERS FROM DIFFERENT BACKGROUND

"When you drive lightweight, fragile sports cars, you drive with a different attitude towards the machinery. 'Well, pip, pip, we turn here.' Those stock car guys go tearing through the esses, and if there's asphalt under the car, OK. Dirt, that's OK, too. Who cares!"

ROCKY MORAN

"Race drivers are schizophrenics ... I'm a completely different person outside of the car."

BUDDY BAKER

"I love this kind of racing, [but] these guys sure change their personalities in race mode. They're like Doberman pinschers with a hand grenade in their mouths."

ROAD RACER BORIS SAID ON NEXTEL CUP DRIVERS

"He was part Elvis, part Santa Claus and part comedian."

PIT REPORTER MATT YOCUM ON 1973 NASCAR CHAMP AND AWARD-WINNING BROADCASTER BENNY PARSONS, WHO PASSED AWAY SHORTLY BEFORE THE START OF THE 2007 SEASON

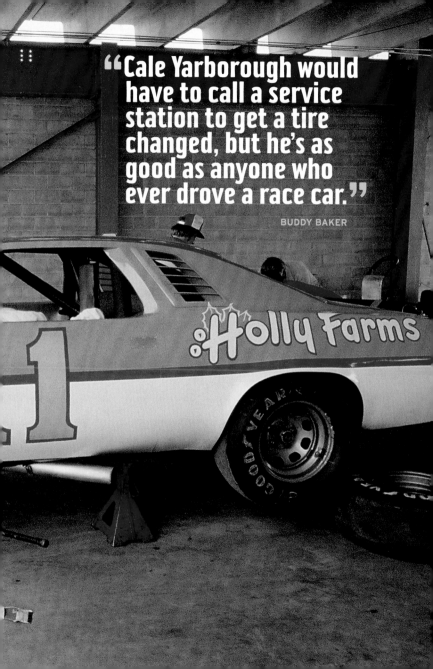

> **"Cale Yarborough would have to call a service station to get a tire changed, but he's as good as anyone who ever drove a race car."**
>
> BUDDY BAKER

"Ernie Irvan could go bear hunting with a switch.
He ain't never afraid."

BUDDY BAKER

"We call him MacGyver.
He can fix anything.
He can build anything.
He's so intense and he's so skilled."

BRENT DEWAR, WHO OVERSEES RACE MARKETING FOR
GENERAL MOTORS, ON ROBBY GORDON

"I'm not as comfortable in front of a camera. I'm not
as comfortable in front of a lot of people. But when
I'm sitting in a car in front of a lot of people, I don't
even realize they're there until it's over, and then you
realize how cool it is that we get to do what we do."

KASEY KAHNE

"When a person comes in and they become a totally
different person over five years, it's hard to have
respect for them or be around that kind of person.
But Jimmie's always been the same."

DALE EARNHARDT JR. ON JIMMIE JOHNSON AFTER HE
WON THE 2006 NEXTEL CUP CHAMPIONSHIP

"You know, when Arnold Palmer came on TV with an old tractor and told me to buy Pennzoil, I bought that, and when Dale Jarrett advertises UPS, I can go along with that, too. But I don't think having an 18-year-old, **somebody who's probably gotten five packages in his life and they were all Girls Gone Wild videos,** tell me what delivery service I should use would have much effect on me."

KYLE PETTY

"I think the only thing you've got to think about is just giving yourself enough time in between sponsorship commitments and deals. You're trying to make the sport better and make your sponsor happy."

KASEY KAHNE ON THE PRESSURE FACED BY THE BIG MONEY IN RACING

"Buy more cases, run more races."

SLOGAN COINED BY BORIS SAID TO ENCOURAGE HIS FANS (THE SAIDHEADS) TO BUY MORE OF THE PEPSI-PRODUCED ENERGY DRINK THAT SPONSORS HIS TEAM

"I told them they better get somebody else, that I didn't know anything about saving gas."

BUDDY BAKER ON BEING ASKED TO DO A TV SPOT FOR CONSERVING FUEL

"I see it on pit road when we make better pit stops and that comes from harder work back at the shop, practicing, testing, trying to get better."

DALE EARNHARDT

"Look at Jeff Burton. Everybody wrote him off like he forgot how to drive."

JEFF GORDON ON THE IMPORTANCE OF HAVING A GOOD CAR AND A GOOD TEAM

"It's no easy task. It's not like you can purchase a race car and motor and head to the track. Everything has to be perfect."

ROGER CARTER II ON READYING HIS NEW TEAM FOR THE 2007 ARCA CIRCUIT

"The thing about it is, all those races we lost, we won this race together. We won it as a team."

DALE EARNHARDT

"We won four races and finished eighth in points. But we had nine DNFs. After blowing up at the second Pocono race, I told Dale I wouldn't hold him to his contract, which had another year, if he wanted to leave, and that we were not giving him the equipment for a driver of his caliber. He said, 'Naw, we're in this together, and we'll fix it together.'"

OWNER RICHARD CHILDRESS, ON THE 1985 TURNING POINT IN THE CAREERS OF DALE EARNHARDT AND RCR ENTERPRISES, WHO WENT ON TO WIN WINSTON CUP TITLES IN 1986 AND 1987

"I don't feel I'm a step above anyone on this team. I'm just another link in the chain."

JEFF GORDON

"I haven't even seen the finish. It is what it is. We were inches or feet or whatever. We were short. It was so close, but it was second. I let it slip away, slip through my fingers, and I'm fine with that. I am very proud of what this team did for me this weekend."

MARK MARTIN, WHO WAS OVERTAKEN BY KEVIN HARVICK AT THE FINISH OF THE 2007 RACE AND REMAINED WINLESS IN 23 STARTS AT THE DAYTONA 500

"You have to remain focused on what you're doing to the exclusion of nearly everything else. There are other cars around you, hoses on the ground, your teammates are on the ground and you have to do everything quickly ... You have to be ready to react to whatever comes up."

LONGTIME CREWMAN BRITT GOODRICH

"The interesting thing is we'd never met each other before we started working with each other. But the level of intensity between us is identical. We're the same age, but he's kind of like a big brother."

TONY STEWART ON CREW CHIEF GREG ZIPADELLI

"When this man tells me it's OK, then I believe everything is OK."

DALE JARRETT, 2000 DAYTONA 500 WINNER, ON CREW CHIEF TODD PARROTT, WHO REPAIRED HIS POLE-WINNING CAR WHICH HAD BEEN DAMAGED IN PRACTICE LESS THAN 24 HOURS BEFORE THE RACE

"Because Ray Evernham went with me."

JEFF GORDON, CREDITING HIS EARLY SUCCESS IN THE WINSTON CUP SERIES TO THE FACT THAT HIS CREW CHIEF CAME WITH HIM FROM THE BUSCH GRAND NATIONAL

"Before a driver starts asking the crew to make changes on the car, he has to figure out how much of the problem is him."

ROCKY MORAN

"We're looking for someone with strength, speed and coordination. People who desire to beat some-one; they have that competitive spirit about them."

BREON KLOPP, WHO HELPS OPERATE THE 5 OFF 5 ON RACE TEAM PERFORMANCE PIT CREW SCHOOL

"You have to be able to shut everything else out. If you're a tire changer, you need to get your five lug nuts off and your five lug nuts on. That's all you have to worry about."

BREON KLOPP

"There are a lot of similarities between playing foot-ball and being a pit crew member. The equipment is heavy, tires are heavy, and you have to be quick. You expend a lot of energy over a short period of time, and you must have good hand-eye coordination."

LONGTIME CREWMAN BRITT GOODRICH

"We just out thunk 'em there at the end."

RICHARD PETTY, CREDITING HIS SEVENTH DAYTONA 500
VICTORY IN 1981 TO CREW CHIEF DALE INMAN'S DECISION
NOT TO CHANGE THE TIRES ON PETTY'S LAST STOP OF THE
DAY

"I don't like people drafting me ... Why draft when
you're fast enough to lead? I leave that stuff alone
and try to get out front. It is very frustrating,
though, when somebody drafts me. It's hard to
shake them off."

MARIO ANDRETTI, WHO WAS MORE USED TO INDY CAR
RACING, ANNOYED BY THE NASCAR TECHNIQUE, DESPITE
WINNING THE 1967 DAYTONA 500

"It looked like a bunch of New York taxicabs when they threw that flag."

TIM FLOCK ON THE START OF THE FIRST SOUTHERN 500,
AT DARLINGTON IN 1950

"The best way to make a small fortune in racing is
to start with a big one."

JUNIOR JOHNSON

"You've started a lot of engines."

FX NASCAR TELEVISION HOST CHRIS MYERS TO ALL-STAR
CHALLENGE GRAND MARSHALL PAMELA ANDERSON

"I've had a lot of success here over the years. Every time someone asks about Pocono they say, 'That's a weird racetrack,' so I guess I just like weird."

DARRELL WALTRIP

"Moonshiners put more time, energy, thought, and love into their cars than any racer ever will. Lose on the track, and you go home. Lose with a load of whiskey, and you go to jail."

JUNIOR JOHNSON, NASCAR LEGEND AND ONE TIME WHISKEY RUNNER

"To win here, you don't have to be the best driver – only crazier than the rest."

BELGIUM'S OLIVIER GENDEBIEN, PRIOR TO THE INAUGURAL DAYTONA CONTINENTAL THREE-HOUR RACE IN 1962, FORERUNNER TO THE 24 HOURS OF DAYTONA (THE RACE INCREASED TO 24 HOURS IN 1966)

"You go from being a big fish in a small pond to a small fish in a big pond."

ALAN KULWICKI ON MAKING THE TRANSITION TO THE NASCAR WINSTON CUP SERIES

"When you pull into Victory Lane, it makes you feel good that you just ruined their day."

JEFF GORDON ON THE FANS WHO BOO HIM

"If NASCAR racing gets any more exciting, I may not be able to stand it."

ROGER STAUBACH, WHO GOT INTO CAR OWNERSHIP WITH FELLOW FORMER DALLAS COWBOYS QUARTERBACK TROY AIKMAN

"A bunch of demons came out when it got dark, I know that much. All hell broke loose after that."

KEVIN HARVICK, WINNER OF THE 2007 DAYTONA 500, ON THE CRASH-FILLED CONCLUSION TO THAT RACE

"Robby's got a little problem going faster under caution than he does under green."

JEFF GORDON, AFTER BEING BEATEN BY ROBBY GORDON AT SONOMA IN 2003

"It's like when your girlfriend breaks up with you, she has to tell all her girlfriends about what's going to happen, but you don't know. That's the way it is here."

KENNY IRWIN JR., DISCUSSING HOW THE DRIVER IS ALWAYS THE LAST TO KNOW HE'S BEING REPLACED

"I don't think our system of provisional starting spots is right. The nature of this sport is competition; to me, you're either fast enough or you don't make the show. Do the Green Bay Packers get a free spot in the playoffs just because they won some Super Bowls?"

DAVE MARCIS

"At this point, I think if I saw someone on the side of the road selling horseshoes, I would stop and buy one."

BOBBY LABONTE, DURING A TOUGH SEASON

"Couldn't hold the bottom. Couldn't hold the top. Couldn't hold him off."

KYLE BUSCH, FRUSTRATED AFTER BEING EDGED OUT (AND SPUN) BY JEFF BURTON AT THE FINISH OF THE 2007 BUSCH SERIES RACE AT LAS VEGAS MOTOR SPEEDWAY

"I feel safer on a racetrack than I do on Houston's freeways."

A.J. FOYT

"He had the fastest car and I had the second fastest. I don't think I could have gotten past him without some kind of break. Personally, I'm glad he ran out of fuel."

RICHARD PETTY, WHO WON THE 1971 DAYTONA 500 AFTER INDY CAR VETERAN A.J. FOYT RAN OUT OF GAS ON LAP 162

"I don't want to argue with my wife about her car – or my driving."

DALE EARNHARDT

"I'm not getting a minivan."

JEFF GORDON, WHEN HIS WIFE WAS EXPECTING THEIR FIRST CHILD

"I'm too damn fat to be climbing fences. I had to do it once, though."

TONY STEWART, AFTER CLIMBING THE CHAIN FENCE FOLLOWING HIS WIN AT DAYTONA IN JULY 2005

"**Geez,** I've got to stop doing those **backflips. They're making me dizzy.**"

CARL EDWARDS ON HIS TRADEMARK CELEBRATION TECHNIQUE

"No such thing as a bad win or a good loss."

WARREN JOHNSON

"If it was easy, you could go out there and you wouldn't have to think."

GEOFFREY BODINE ON THE VARIETY OF TRACKS ON THE NASCAR CIRCUIT

"To finish first, you must first finish."

RICK MEARS

"I still get the check. I still get the trophy, and I'm still the most recent winner until we go to Daytona."

GREG BIFFLE, WHO WON THE SEASON-ENDING FORD 400 AT HOMESTEAD-MIAMI SPEEDWAY FOR THE THIRD YEAR IN A ROW IN 2006, BUT HAS ALWAYS HAD THOSE WINS OVER-SHADOWED BY THE CROWNING OF THE SEASON'S CHAMPION

"It's not time to panic yet. It almost is."

MICHAEL WALTRIP, JUST TWO RACES INTO THE 2007 SEASON, ON HIS TEAM'S SLOW START IN TOYOTAS

"You win some, lose some and wreck some."

DALE EARNHARDT

"Fireball Roberts, perhaps the most nearly perfect of all stock-car drivers, is dead and it is like awaking to find a mountain suddenly gone."

CHARLOTTE NEWS WRITER MAX MUHLEMAN ON THE 1964
DEATH OF NASCAR'S FIRST SUPERSTAR, GLENN "FIREBALL"
ROBERTS

"In a race, I'm always scared, but what I fear most is fire."

GLENN "FIREBALL" ROBERTS (WHOSE NICKNAME CAME
FROM HIS SPEED AS A BASEBALL PITCHER). ROBERTS DIED
OF HIS BURNS AFTER A FIERY CRASH AT DARLINGTON IN
1964

"I'm doing what I like best. This is my life, and I'm having too much fun to retire now."

TINY LUND, NINE DAYS BEFORE DYING IN A CRASH AT
TALLEDEGA IN 1975

"I don't think he's going to get out of that one."

RICHARD PETTY, RADIOING IN TO HIS CREW AFTER THE
HORRIFIC CRASH THAT CLAIMED THE LIFE OF TINY LUND
AT THE 1975 TALLADEGA 500

"Racing is dangerous, but I've been in a lot worse
situations as a pipe fitter."

NEIL BONNETT, WHO LATER DIED IN A CRASH AT DAYTONA
WHILE ATTEMPTING TO COME BACK FROM RETIREMENT

"Undoubtedly, this is one of the toughest announce-
ments I've personally had to make: After the
accident in Turn four at the end of the Daytona
500, we've lost Dale Earnhardt."

NASCAR PRESIDENT MIKE HELTON, CONFIRMING THAT
DALE EARNHARDT HAD BEEN KILLED IN A CRASH LATE
IN THE 2001 DAYTONA 500

"To win more championships and stay alive in this sport, it's very, very hard and it's hard to understand how it works."

DALE EARNHARDT

cover: Todd Warshaw/Getty Images; title page: Jamie Squire/Getty Images for NASCAR; 8 Jonathan Ferrey/Getty Images; 13 Getty Images for NASCAR; 18 Darrell Ingham/Getty Images; 24 Jonathan Ferrey/Getty Images; 34 Jonathan Ferrey/Getty Images; 39 Jonathan Ferrey/Getty Images; 43 Donald Miralle/Allsport/Getty Images; 48 Jamie Squire/Getty Images; 53 Mathew Stockman/Getty Images; 55 John Ferrey/Allsport/Getty Images; 61 Michael Rougier/Time & Life Pictures/Getty Images; 63 Chris Graythen/Getty Images; 66 Jonathan Ferrey/Getty Images for NASCAR; 69 Sam Sharpe/The Sharpe Image/Corbis; 75 Ronaldo Schemidt/AFP/Getty Images; 76 Darrell Ingham/Getty Images for NASCAR; 82 Jamie Squire/Getty Images for NASCAR; 87 Nick Laham/Getty Images; 92 Robert Laberge/Getty Images; 96 David Taylor/Allsport/ Getty Images; 103 Bettmann/Corbis; 104 Hulton Archive/Getty Images; 109 Jamie Squire/Getty Images for NASCAR; 116 Bettman/Corbis; 120 Todd Warshaw/Getty Images for NASCAR; 124 Doug Benc/Getty Images; 128 Todd Warshaw/Getty Images for NASCAR; 132 Darrell Ingham /Allsport/Getty Images; 139 Bettman/Corbis; 144 Jonathan Ferrey/Getty Images for NASCAR; 148 Focus on Sport/Getty Images; 154 Nick Laham/Getty Images; 155 Harry How/Getty Images; 160 Rusty Jarrett/Getty Images; 165 Nick Laham/Getty Images for NASCAR; 170 David Taylor/Allsport/Getty Images

Eric Zweig is a sports historian and managing editor with Dan Diamond and Associates, consulting publishers to the National Hockey League. He has written for many Canadian newspapers and is the author or editor of dozens of sports books, including three other "Quotes and Quips" titles for Firefly Books. As a boy, he watched stock car races at the Barrie Speedway and cheered for Number 36.